Tales from
WILLOWSHADE
Farm: An Island Woman's NOTEBOOK

WILLOWSHADE FARM
TRYON, P.E.I.
E. K. HOWATT JR.
BERRIES, FRUIT, HONEY

Tales from
Willowshade Farm:
An Island Woman's Notebook

Betty Howatt

Illustrated by
Dale McNevin

The Acorn Press
Charlottetown
2003

Tales from Willowshade Farm: An Island Woman's Notebook
Text © 2003 by Betty Howatt
Illustrations © 2003 by Dale McNevin
ISBN 1-894838-07-6
Second Printing, 2004

Editing: Marian Bruce
Manuscript preparation: Ruth Robins-Jeffery, Charmin White,
Laura Mair
Science consultants: Lawson Drake, Donna Giberson,
Ian MacQuarrie
Design: Matthew MacKay
Printing: Hignell Book Printing

The Acorn Press gratefully acknowledges the support of Molly
Colburn and Fred Gross; The Canada Council for the Arts'
Emerging Publisher Program; and the Prince Edward Island
Department of Community and Cultural Affairs' Cultural
Development Program.

National Library of Canada Cataloguing in Publication

Howatt, Betty, 1929–
    Tales from Willowshade Farm : an Island woman's
notebook / Betty Howatt.

ISBN 1-894838-07-61. Natural history—Prince Edward Island.
2. Gardening—Prince Edward Island. 3. Farm life—Prince
Edward Island. I. Title.

S522.C3H69 2003   508.717   C2003-902907-7

The Acorn Press
PO Box 22024
Charlottetown, Prince Edward Island
Canada C1A 9J2

www.acornpresscanada.com

Printed on 100% recycled paper.

For Everett
and our families
and
in loving memory
of
Eleanor Wheler
and
Elaine Harrison

Contents

Creatures of the Wild

In the Garden

Feasts from the Farm

Acknowledgements

These stories have been compiled from broadcasts presented on CBC Charlottetown's radio program "Mainstreet."

Thanks are due to those who recorded and produced them, beginning in 1995 with Sheryl MacKay, Nils Ling, and Whit Carter. Andrew Morrow served longer than any other. The work is now being done by Eva O'Hanley and Matt Rainnie, assisted by Joe Gillis and Richie Bulger. I am truly grateful.

Betty Howatt

The Trees of Willowshade Farm

Willowshade Farm, where I live with my husband Everett, runs from the shore of the Tryon River on the east, through meadows and uplands to our woodlot on the west. Through our kitchen and living room windows, we have a view of hedges, trees, and fields sloping down to the mouth of the river and the Northumberland Strait. Most of the year, the colours of the water on the Strait change continually with the falling and rising tides, or with the swirling lines of currents on a hot summer's day. In winter, the fields, river, and Strait become one great expanse of white. Only the hedges around our lawns and the hedgerows around the fields help to keep the view in perspective.

Over the years, Everett and I have planted thousands of trees on the farm — spruce and pine for hedgerows and shelter belts, different varieties of nut trees, walnuts, butternuts, hazelnuts, edible chestnuts, heartnuts, pecans, and hickories. Everett's grandfather used to say, "Plant your hedge before you go a-courting." It didn't happen quite that way with us, although Everett did have me help him plant the first of our hedges two years before we married in 1952. And the spring before we were married, I helped plant pine trees on a May holiday weekend. Everett told the neighbours he wanted to be sure I'd be able to do the work required on the farm!

The property on which we live was settled by Everett's Howatt ancestors in 1783. They built their first small house close to the Tryon River, as access was then by boat. In about 1820, they moved to a larger house, close to a road that led to Tryon Point, but still within a few hundred yards of the river and the Strait. In the late 1800s, the Howatts planted a black willow tree near the east end of the house, giving rise to the name of Willowshade Farm.

When we came to live on the farm, the black willow was already quite large, and leaning strongly towards the house. A few years later, it began to split, as these old willows are prone to do. Everett persuaded a blacksmith in the neighbouring village to make a long auger and three equally long threaded rods. The man thought we were crazy to spend $10 to save an old willow tree. After much hard work, Everett got the rods through both parts of the tree, and used metal plates as washers under the nuts. That kept things together while our daughter and son were growing up, and provided a place for a tree house. Gradually, though, the rods were pulled through; the very large limbs braced themselves on the ground, and the tree continued to spread itself far and wide. Then came the time when, for our safety and that of the house, we had to begin removing it. A white birch, about as tall as a person, had started to grow inside one half of the old willow, with the main root running down the trunk and into the ground at the base. Over the next few years, we removed most of the remaining half of the willow in large chunks. The birch tree remained unharmed, perched on top of what looked like an aerial root. We were able to gently persuade the root to lie down enough to cover it with soil, though this left the tree at quite an angle. Over the past few years, through judicious pruning, the birch has become almost upright. After piling more soil over the root, we planted sage, wormwood, and a fiddlehead fern at the base.

We grow fruits and vegetables for sale on our farm, and our customers usually refer to us as "Howatts' Fruit Farm." But, even though the old black willow is almost gone, there are others to continue to justify the name of Willowshade Farm. Everett has always liked weeping willows, so in the 1950s I bought him one for Father's Day. It didn't grow very well, but we were able to root some cuttings from it and plant a number of golden weeping willows around our house yard in 1967. They are large trees now, with graceful branches sweeping the ground (annoying those who mow the grass) and providing food and shelter for the birds.

Everett and I come by our love of trees honestly. Everett's father and grandfather both planted a variety of trees around the yard and fields. West of our house is a tall horse-chestnut tree, which was large when Everett was a youngster. To the east, between the farm yard and our vegetable field, there are more chestnuts, beautiful trees, which were started by my father, Grandpa King, in his garden in Charlottetown. After Everett and I married, we brought those trees to the farm. Grandpa King also started the oaks we've planted in various places.

In spite of the Howatt love of trees, there were few trees left on this particular piece of land when Everett and I moved here in 1952. What had happened was that this property had been severed from Grandpa's land when a Howatt daughter married in about 1880. The property finally went on the market in 1950, and Everett bought it back into the family name. We immediately began planting spruce and pine trees to mark off and give shelter to the various fields. Ironically, it was about that time that farming became agri-business: the provincial government began subsidizing the removal of hedgerows to enlarge fields for large machinery.

Before we were married, Everett had begun planting standard

(large-growing) apple trees, adding more trees, different growing types and more varieties as the years went on. At one time, we had more than sixty varieties, including a number of heritage ones. With pears, plums, and cherries, we eventually had fifteen acres of fruit trees. There were always enough relatives and friends to help out at picking time. Then buying habits changed. Supermarkets came on the scene, providing fresh fruit year-round; U-pick orchards came into prominence, and our large trees did not lend themselves to that form of harvesting. As well, with many women working away from home, the demand declined for fruit for home-canning and preserving. As a result, Everett has begun to remove the standard trees and concentrate on a section of semi-standards more easily cared for. At one point, we planted a row of plum trees of a type once grown freely in older orchards in our area. That was a bad idea. The plum trees were very thorny and very prone to black knot, and didn't grow well in the sod headland. Fortunately, the plum trees gradually died out, although suckers, complete with black knot, continued to appear for years. New plum trees, planted in 1994, are now producing. Our cherry trees, relatively short-lived, are continually being renewed. We have only a few pear trees left for fresh fruit in season and have not replaced the older canning varieties.

Some trees have been on the farm for generations. The black locusts have managed to survive, in spite of the disapproval of my father, Grandpa King. They are thorny, ragged trees, and very late in leafing out. When Grandpa King used to come for a visit in the spring to help with the cleaning-up around the farm, he would invariably declare the trees dead and say it was time to remove them. The trees are still here, and they still produce bunches of fragrant, pea-like blossoms in early summer. When the time does come to remove these old trees, they will have to be handled carefully; pieces of wire are embedded in the trunks from the time many years ago when they were living fence posts, enclosing a calf yard. The furrowed locust bark provides insect treats for birds, as well as places to store seeds from our feeders. On occasion, sunflower seeds sprout in the bark. One year, a sunflower managed to grow about three feet high, far above our heads. At various times, we see in the locust trees Blue Jays, Chickadees, Blackbirds, Starlings, Warblers, Finches, Downy and Hairy Woodpeckers, Flickers, Crows, and many kinds of Sparrows. The locust trees are close to the west window in our bedroom, so we usually begin our day by checking the activity there.

The chestnut trees east of our house provide another kind of pleasure. Underneath them is a place I call my outdoor classroom, where people from kindergarten to Elderhostel age have gathered over the years to learn natural history or the story of local settlement. That place is also a haven for us, where we can simply sit and absorb the beauty all around us. The chestnut trees are close enough to our on-farm-market that I can take a break underneath them on fine days. Our customers will often join me. It's a place that gives rest and refreshment to a weary soul. We can look over the fields to the river and the Strait beyond, listen to the songs of birds and the whisper of the trees, catch the scent of strawberries and clover, watch seagulls wheeling overhead, and sometimes even spot ospreys and eagles in the act of catching a fish.

Our kind of farming requires a great deal of hard physical labour. Being able to live in a place of such peace and beauty helps make the work worthwhile. I have said more than once that without such treats for the spirit, I wouldn't be able to continue.

Without our trees, of course, much of what we treasure on our farm would be lost. They give us so much—shelter year-round, shade in summer, homes for birds, and food for our bodies and our spirits. We cherish the trees on Willowshade Farm.

WILLOWSHADE FARM
TRYON, P.E.I.
E. K. HOWATT JR.
BERRIES, FRUIT, HONEY

The Howatt Farm

Grandpa's and Granny's Story

When Grandpa and Granny married in 1921, they had already beaten the odds against their very survival. Both had come through bouts of serious illness, he with tuberculosis and she with the Spanish flu. On his return from overseas, after being in the trenches of France during the First World War, he was said to have "weak lungs," and was given medical orders to sleep out-of-doors for a year. Sleeping outside during summer is not a real hardship in Prince Edward Island, but winter weather is another matter. To comply with the order, he set up a ridge tent in the orchard next to his parents' house. I saw an old snapshot of that tent a few years ago. It had board flaps on the sides that could be let down as desired. The treatment seems harsh, but it must have worked: his health improved.

Granny, then known as Clara Thomas, had gone, as did many young Maritimers, to the "Boston States" to find employment. She was simply following several of her sisters who were already there. One of them stayed all her working life; the others eventually returned and married on the Island. Clara worked in a wealthy home as companion to two young family members. Their father was a politician, and their mother was involved in related social affairs, so Clara became a dependable constant in the children's lives. With them, she took piano, tennis, and swimming lessons, and learned to canoe at the family's posh summer home. She was quite content and had no intention of leaving.

Then fate, in the guise of the Spanish flu, intervened. Clara became very ill. I remember her telling me the only thing her stomach wouldn't reject was champagne, something completely foreign to her teetotal Methodist upbringing. But she began to recover, and when her doctor in Boston recommended that she take an extended holiday to recuperate fully, she came back to her parents' home to do just that, intending to return to her post when fit.

Her own mother, Granny Thomas, was a midwife and practical nurse, whose skills were well-respected by the local physician. As Clara's health improved, she began helping out in the area; one of the homes to which she went was the Howatts'. Mrs. Howatt was ill and required some help. One of the Howatt boys was Everett King, Sr. When he and Clara became acquainted, that was the end of her plans to return to Boston. Instead, she married Grandpa one cold January day at five o'clock in the morning. That early hour gave them enough time to be driven (by horse and sleigh, of course) to the boat train that would take them to Moncton for their honeymoon. People in the district remembered that day well, because of another memorable event—the local forge burned down the same morning.

Grandpa's father and two brothers were still on the farm where he had grown up, so there wasn't really a place for him. Through the Soldiers' Settlement Board, he obtained a loan to buy fifty-one acres of land (of which ten acres were woods) and build a house and barn. The young couple must have been happy with their farm: they called it "Perfection." The house was very modern for the times, a bungalow in a countryside where most homes were of the usual large style found in farming districts, many of them added to for an extended family. The basement, which later figured in their way of making a living, was partly above-ground, so instead of the usual dark cellar, they had light from the windows.

Making a living on a small acreage took hard work and extra initiative. Grandpa and Granny decided to go into the poultry business. They developed top-quality White Leghorn hens, which they used as the basis for a hatchery and broiler business. When the Experimental Farm in Charlottetown developed a program of testing hens for egg production, Grandpa joined the program, and one member of his flock was the first registered hen in the world.

The incubators and brooders were in the basement of the house. Kerosene lamps, which were tricky to manage, provided heat for the equipment. Everett says the safety of the business depended

on Granny's nose—her ability to smell a lamp that wasn't burning properly in the basement, even when she was upstairs. Everett also remembers helping to candle the eggs. This took place a few days after the eggs went into an incubator, by which time you could separate fertile from infertile eggs. Granny mixed the infertile eggs with very fine corn meal, baked them in large flat pans, and then cooled and crumbled the mixture to feed the newly hatched chicks until they could eat coarser grains. Once hatched, chicks that customers had ordered would be packed in cartons and hauled to the train station in Albany. Those that remained would go into brooders until they were large enough to move into one of the small buildings in the farmyard.

The hatchery business continued successfully for a number of years, but came to an end when government began demanding a separate building for each part of the operation. Granny and Grandpa decided it would be too costly a venture, so they closed down their operation. By the time I came to know them, there wasn't a hen left on the farm, and there hasn't been one since. In the meantime, though, people began looking for U-pick strawberries, and Granny and Grandpa planted more land in berries.

Granny and Grandpa worked hard to provide for their three children, and continued as full working partners for a number of years after Everett returned to the farm from a seven-year absence. When Everett and I married and expanded the range of products grown here, they continued to help. They loved their farm, no doubt, but they also recognized the constant amount of work needed to keep it going. Granny even suggested I'd be better off if I went back to teaching, athough she really believed women should be at home to look after the children.

In spite of all the hard work and low pay, I don't think Granny would have preferred the life she had planned to have in Boston. She and Grandpa enjoyed many loving years together before he died at the relatively young age of seventy-five. She lived many more years, until she was just short of her hundredth birthday. They both now rest in a cemetery overlooking the Tryon River.

Houses with Backstairs

From the time I was very small, I felt a house that had backstairs was a very special place, and that I would like to live in one some day. Eventually I did, several of them in fact, but they belonged to other people.

The farmhouse where I spent so many happy, busy summers had backstairs in its early years, but when my uncle married, my grandparents moved into a section of the house downstairs, and access from part of the upper floor was removed. During that same growing-up time, one of my sisters and I would sometimes visit a great-aunt, whose house had a backstairs. What fun! The kitchen wall was covered with vertical wooden boards, darkened over the years by varnish and smoke from the wood stove. Looking carefully to the left of the stove, you could see a thumb-latch and handle sticking out of the kitchen wall. That marked a door that opened to reveal a set of stairs between two walls. There was no light in the stairwell; any light had to come from the rooms above, as the door in the kitchen wall was kept closed most of the time. On a cold winter's night, it would be opened flat against the wall to allow heat from the stove to give a hope of warmth to the bedrooms. What made the stairs exciting and a bit scary for us youngsters was the sight of Cousin Joe's "tin leg" in the corner of his room, just where we could spot it as we reached the top of the stairs.

Cousin Joe was my grand-aunt's bachelor son, who lived with her. Children in those days did not call older people by their Christian names without using some form of honorific, so we called him Cousin Joe. We had lots of cousins, in the same way we had five grandmothers. Try explaining that! Cousin Joe had lost a leg on a battlefield in France during the Great War. His prosthesis, which went halfway up his thigh, was a very heavy, awkward affair, requiring a full body harness; he never seemed to have much comfort with it. At different times, he acquired new ones to try to improve his lot, so it was usual for him to have two "tin legs" in the house at one time. Even with such a disability, he carried on farming, and I can still see him as he walked behind a team of horses that he was about to hitch to a piece of machinery, trying to keep up with them with his hop-skip step. The leg he used that day would wear a work sock and a work boot; the spare one standing in the corner would have a dress sock and dress shoe. We children called the two his "Monday leg" and his "Sunday leg."

It has taken me longer to explain that than it did for us to squeak and skitter and scramble up those stairs, past the bedrooms, into the hall, down the front stairs, and out into the room where our grand-aunt sat quietly, watching us play.

When I taught in rural schools I boarded in several homes that had backstairs. In the first of these only the hired man used the stairs to get to his quarters above the back kitchen. No playing on the stairs there. In the second house there was a small room between stairs that became my winter bedroom for two years. The rooms in the two main parts of the house had ceilings about twelve feet high. Two families lived there—an older man and his wife, as well as their son and his wife and children. Each family had its own kitchen stove. Fires in the parlours were rarely lit. The only other heat in that big house came from an oil stove in the hall at the foot of the main stairs. As winter came on, my high-ceilinged bedroom became cold, so I moved into that little low-ceilinged room between stairs, which by comparison was downright cozy. My landlady would make sure there was a hot water bottle in my bed at night, and I was quite content.

Before Everett and I were married, we planned to build a house near his parents, on land they farmed. However, there was a house across the road, built about 1820 by Everett's ancestors. The first Howatts came to Prince Edward Island in 1775, and settled in Tryon in 1783. In the late 1800s, through being left to a daughter, the house passed out of the Howatt name and was owned by several other families. Before we started building, what was left of the original house came on the market, and Everett bought it.

At one time, that house had backstairs. I saw them often enough

after I came to live in Tryon and began visiting families that lived in the little house.

In the early years of its life, that house was home to an extended family. We have a copy of an "Agreement" from 1835, wherein an older man and his wife made a legal covenant with two bachelor sons as to management of the farm and the living arrangements within the house. On paper, everything was divided, including the beds and bedding, pots and pans. Nothing was left to chance. The parents had the western part of the house, the sons the eastern. I imagine that was so the sons would be closer to the barns, better able to keep an eye on things going on there. The father was to be semi-retired, and had no more need for visiting the barns in the middle of the night to tend to ailing animals or sows about to have a litter of pigs.

It was the eastern part that contained the backstairs, leading up to two bedrooms. What Everett remembers best about that part were the wide stone steps to the cellar below. Now, steps, stairs, and back bedrooms are all gone. The unthinkable happened through a strange set of circumstances. I lost "my" backstairs.

The family from whom Everett bought the house and farm had a hard time trying to make a living from what they could produce.

The couple, who had two small sons, decided they needed help on the farm, so they hired a young man from the district. Cash was scarce. Instead of paying monthly wages, the couple made a deal whereby the young man would work for room and board and tobacco until the fall, when the couple would sell animals and crops, and could pay him in one lump sum.

The time for reckoning arrived. But the crops had been poor and there was still no ready money for wages. What to do? Answer: cut the eastern end off the house and help the hired man move it onto a plot of unclaimed land between river and road. He was planning to marry, and, being a jack-of-all-trades, he was able to fix up a home for himself and his bride. A house in lieu of wages!

And that's how I missed out on having a home with backstairs.

Marshes and Marsh Plants

According to government survey maps, there are about 600 acres of marshland along the Tryon River and its branches. These marshes have been important to human life from the arrival of the first native peoples, to the present day. Based on deeds drawn about 1820, our farm in Tryon West contains five acres of marsh, but shoreline changes since then may have altered that figure.

When Granny Howatt was growing up in North Tryon, she helped her father harvest hay on marshes that were part of their property, though actually across the river from their farm. She remembers that the marshes were designated, not by acreage, but by the amount of hay that could reasonably be expected from each section—a two-stack marsh or a three-stack marsh. A widowed aunt had a five-stack marsh. That this hay was available was due to the efforts of the Acadians. After British forces expelled them from their dyked marshlands in Nova Scotia, they set up the same type of farming on what then was called Île St. Jean. Another forced move in the 1750s left land and marshes to the settlers that the British brought or encouraged to come. Granny Howatt's grandfather was one of the disbanded British soldiers given a grant of land on the acreage that Samuel Holland received as payment in 1767 for his work of surveying the Island.

Granny was one of seven sisters. With no brother to help on the farm, the lot fell to her. With her father she would row across the river, cut the marsh hay with a scythe, and pile it on makeshift platforms, where it would stay until the river ice was thick enough to haul the hay home. Granny told me one of her greatest worries was having a mouse run up her leg. She didn't like mice, and there were usually lots of them around the marsh. It is no wonder she was happy to leave the farm and go to work in the "Boston States."

Besides the marsh hay, many other types of plants grew on the marsh. Among them were what we call bulrushes, but are really cattails (the true bulrush is another family). There are numerous species of cattails in the world, including two in Canada: *Typha latifolia*, broad-leaved with male and female sections closely joined, and *Typha angustifolia*, with a narrower leaf and a distinct separation between male and female flowers. A child visiting our farm once described the seed head as a wiener on a stick that was browned over a campfire. The children in that group were familiar with the story of Moses in the bulrushes; I explained to them the plants in the Bible story were really papyrus, but the two types of plants had some similar uses. The strap-like leaves were used for weaving floor mats, chair seats, roof coverings, and containers such as Moses' cradle. In England, the cattail is known as the reed mace, which is the meaning of the Greek word *typha*. In earlier years it was one of the rushes placed on floors and replaced with fresh ones as needed.

Our native peoples used the plants as food in all stages of growth. In spring, before the pollen appeared, they boiled the green spikes and ate them like corn on the cob. The hearts from the early stem are said to resemble asparagus; in fact, the Europeans call it "Cossack asparagus." The natives mixed the pollen with flour to make a high-protein food, or stored it for use as talcum powder. They ate the sprouts on the rootstalk raw or cooked, and made flour from the rootstalks, which were pounded in water, the fibres removed, and the starchy flour allowed to settle. After several more washings, the flour could be used immediately or stored for later use.

If we add to all that the uses for the fluffy seed heads—as mattress and pillow stuffings, antiseptic dressings, particularly for burns, and disposable diaper linings, biodegradable and environmentally friendly—then we know why the cattails were so highly regarded.

In Europe, the brown heads, dipped in tallow, were used as torches. Smoky though they might be, these were the rush lights and *flambeaux* we read of in historical stories. Many of us remember, as children, making torches by dipping the heads into kerosene oil. Youngsters whooping and hollering around the yard with flaming torches in their hands certainly would not be allowed today. Everett recalls one time he and his friends got into trouble by using bulrush heads that were too mature. Some of the heads broke off, leaving seeds inside the kerosene barrel from which Grandpa filled the lamps in the incubators and brooders of the chicken hatchery. There was, according to Everett, "one hell of a row." My husband doesn't often use words like that, so it must have been bad, for Grandpa rarely lost his temper.

Another plant of note, a very tall one, also grows on the Tryon marsh. It is a reed grass, *Phragmites*, from the Greek, meaning a fence or screen because of its hedge-like growth. Fossil evidence in Europe indicates that this is one of the oldest grasses known, with family members found worldwide. This one, *P. australis*, is widespread in Canada and the United States. It grows in fresh or brackish marshes, like the places on the Tryon marsh where small streams of fresh water enter the saltier water of the river. One theory in this area is that the early Acadian settlers planted it to grow their own thatching materials. In Britain, people used reeds for roofing, fencing, and making furniture and boats (coracles, which consisted of a reed frame covered with hide).

To think of reed grass only in the dry form may cause us to overlook its many uses as food. In early spring and fall, the roots are very starchy, and native peoples of North America treated them in the same way as the cattails. They peeled the reeds, and either dried them or pounded them in water, removed the fibres, and washed out the starch. In early summer, the stems, while still green and fleshy, were cut, dried, and pounded into powder. This was moistened enough to form balls that were roasted over the fire, just as we roast marshmallows. In the fall, the tiny seeds could be ground into flour or made into gruel. That was truly working hard for daily bread.

Reed grass is a very striking plant. I measured some stems that were ten feet high. The leaves are long and strap-shaped, something like gladiolus leaves, and the flower head is a beautiful plume. It has become fashionable to use reed grass in designer gardens, as accents in the section devoted to bog plants. There haven't been many generations between reed grass as food plants and reed grass as fancy plants.

A Tale of a Tail

In my school days, a poem in our reader described a fight between a pair of stuffed animals, a gingham dog, and a calico cat who "ate each other up." Two observers, an old Dutch clock and a Chinese plate, told the tale to the narrator, who takes pains after each verse to remind us:

> *I wasn't there; I simply state*
> *What was told to me by the Chinese plate*

What I am going to tell you now is a story that an older friend declares to be true. It explains how a certain family, which later became prominent in all aspects of Island life, happened to settle in a certain district. My informant heard the story from a man who lived in that district.

The year was about 1760. The British and French had been at war, and the British were in control. The Acadians who had been living on Île St. Jean—the French name for the Island—were dispersed. Some managed to reach the western part of the Island, and some were deported.

A small French vessel was sailing down the Northumberland Strait. On board were two Scotsmen, the Scots and French being allied against the British just then. For some reason, the Scots got into an argument with the French sailors, who overpowered them, dumped them into an empty puncheon, fastened the top, and threw the puncheon overboard.

> *Now mind, I'm only telling you*
> *What the old Dutch clock declares is true.*

A puncheon is a very large barrel used on board ship to hold any kind of supplies, including drinking water, so we'll not question the presence of an empty puncheon so readily to hand.

But when I tell this story, some people ask, "Why throw the men overboard, why not knock them on the head and get rid of them?" My theory is this: other people probably knew that the Scotsmen were on board, and questions might be asked someday as to their whereabouts. The Frenchmen would be able to reply, "They were in fine fighting trim the last time we saw them, before they boarded a little vessel heading toward the shore of Île St. Jean. Technically speaking, that would be correct.

The little puncheon vessel did indeed head for the shore. The wind and the currents took it landward, and the falling tide left it high and dry in an area simply known as the South Shore. The two men were alive, but stuck in a big barrel with no means of escape.

Don't fancy I exaggerate —
I got my news from the Chinese plate.

A short distance inland were farms that the Acadians had settled but were forced to abandon. Most of their farm animals had been taken to Charlottetown to feed the British garrison there. Most animals, but not all. Some of the cattle had managed to escape the round-up and were living wild. Cattle like to have—need to have— salt in their diet. To get salt, those almost-wild animals would go to the shore, where spray from the Strait had salted the vegetation. In addition, long windrows of salty seaweed often collected along the high-tide line.

It was on this shore that the puncheon came to rest. After pushing out the large bung (stopper) in the side of the puncheon, the men could peer out and see cattle approaching. Cattle being very inquisitive, they began nosing around this strange, inanimate object. Then one of the men shoved his hand through the bung hole, caught a tail, and hung on.

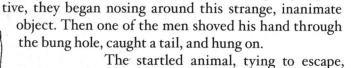

The startled animal, tying to escape, went galumping down the shore with the puncheon thumping and bumping behind it. Gradually, the rough treatment loosened the hoops holding the staves in place, and the men managed to move enough staves to give them an escape hatch.

After their escape, the two Scotsmen eventually took up residence at one of the abandoned farms, found wives, and lived long, fruitful lives. To this day, many of their descendants live on the Island.

Believe it or not, that is the story as told to me. It's one of my husband's favourite tales.

> *The old Dutch clock it told me so,*
> *And that is how I came to know.*

WILLOWSHADE FARM
TRYON, P.E.I.
E. K. HOWATT JR.
BERRIES, FRUIT, HONEY

My Younger Years

The Outhouse Affair

After the Blitz in London during the Second World War, the British government sent about 200,000 British children to Canada, Australia, New Zealand, and South Africa. Twenty-five of these children came to Prince Edward Island. One of them, a girl named Brenda, lived on the farm of relatives with whom I spent most of my summer holidays when I was a girl. Brenda was several years older than I, and, coming from a crowded area near a big city, much wiser in the ways of the world, particularly where boys were concerned.

The term "culture shock" wasn't in vogue then, but I think she must have experienced it, in spades. To leave the lights, the hustle and bustle, and end up in rural PEI must have been a shock. No electricity, no running water, no cars, and, because of the lay of the land, few other farmsteads to be seen—that was the situation when she arrived. However, she was quite prepared to work, and learned how to do many things around the farm, even how to milk cows. The big problem, for her, was evening entertainment—or the lack thereof. She was not accustomed to going to bed as early as the farm family did. For her, evening was the time for playing in the streets with her friends. On the farm, on the other hand, we rarely left home in the evening, and never after 7 P.M. Our family had to rise early to bring the cows from the pasture, milk them, and carry the milk cans to the gate by 7 A.M., before the milk hauler arrived to take the milk to the cheese factory. As a general rule, we went to bed about 8:30 P.M., unless we were going to a church-related affair. Other events in the community, such as "times"—parties where there might be dancing—were not approved. In the only autograph book I have, my uncle wrote one summer:

May your life be filled with sunshine,
And gladdened by romances,
But take advice from one who knows
And avoid the country dances!

I loved that uncle dearly, and heeded his advice. Most of the time.

During those years, a group of travelling evangelists from the United States, known locally as the "Go Preachers," set up a large tent—the Gospel tent— every summer in the next district. The evangelists held a series of evening meetings, which we were allowed to attend. Actually, the services were more in the line of entertainment for the young people who gathered there. Certainly there was lots of preaching, mostly of the hellfire-and-damnation variety, but it was the singing we enjoyed. It was accompanied by a small, portable pump organ, usually drowned out by the enthusiastic—but not necessarily musical—voices from the crowd.

One night when there was no "preaching," Brenda and I went to bed at 8:30 P.M., but couldn't settle down. Our yammering annoyed the folks in bed in the adjoining room. "Keep quiet! Pipe down!" We decided to go out to the outhouse. That was a legitimate reason, or rather, an acceptable one, for leaving the house. As we went out the kitchen door, my Grandpa's steeple clock on the mantel shelf struck 9. We were dressed in our light cotton pyjamas, barefoot, with a flashlight for courage.

As on many farmsteads of those years, there was a separate building for almost every operation on the farm. My great-grandfather had settled on that land in 1863, and over the years the number of buildings had grown to include a hen house, pig house, sheep barn, forge, well-house, combination separator house and wood-shed, carriage house/granary, and a calf house next to the main barn. The barn housed the horses and cows on either side of a big floor where the hay wagon could be driven in; beyond the cow stables was a shed for manure storage. All of these were enclosed by a fence, with a gate leading to the road that ran behind the main buildings. The outhouse was tucked between the carriage house and the calf house.

Brenda and I sat in the outhouse for a little while, talking, until we became chilly and decided it was time to get back to bed. We opened the door. To our surprise, a large dark muzzle poked

through the opening. We quickly shut the door. We realized that our curious visitor was the new driving mare. My uncle had planned to hitch her first thing after chores in the morning, and, to save the time it would take to bring her from the pasture, he had left her loose in the yard, able to go in and out of the stable as she willed. We had been warned to stay away from this mare, as she wasn't used to us, and was said to be quite skittish.

We became skittish as well. We didn't dare venture out while she was nearby, so we sat down to wait for her to leave. Then we decided to sing, loudly; someone in the house might hear, and anyway it would keep our spirits up. So sing we did, mostly the songs we had been singing in the Gospel tent: "Life Is Like a Mountain Railroad," "Will Your Anchor Hold?" and "Pass Me Not O Gentle Saviour." The next line in that last piece is "Hear my humble cry," but there was nothing humble in the way we sang those hymns and many more. We opened the outhouse door. The mare was still there. The fun was gone. We were cold, and we had turned off the flashlight to save the batteries. We had to do something! We changed tactics. This time, we kept quiet for a while. Finally, we heard the mare walk off. We ran like mad to the separator house, kitty-corner from us and halfway to the farmhouse. The mare heard us and reached the separator house door just as we shut it. Another period of waiting. Finally, she moved away again. Then we made a mad dash to the veranda, the mare just behind us as we raced into the house. Just as Grandpa's clock struck 11 P.M. We had been outside two hours.

Everyone else in the house was sound asleep, so we decided not to say a word about our adventure. But the truth will out. Not long after, my uncle was at the village on business. He met a neighbour who had been driving by while Brenda and I were singing loudly— so loudly we didn't hear his horse and wagon. He certainly heard us. "What," he asked my uncle, "was going on?" When my uncle got home, he asked us the same question, and the whole story came out.

Brenda eventually went back to England. I wonder if she is ever reminded of that night in the outhouse. I am. Especially when I hear "Life Is Like a Mountain Railroad."

Social Life in the Country

In pre-television days, the Most Important social occasion of the year was the School Christmas Concert. The teacher's reputation was based on two factors: her ability to "keep order" and the quality of the Christmas concert she produced. All pupils had to take part, and be seen taking part, even if it was only pulling the curtain across the front of the stage. The teacher was producer, director, costume designer, and general facilitator. The costumes were very basic, made from crepe paper, poster paints, old items of clothing. Sometimes the older pupils or a parent or two would help make costumes, and the parents would help keep things running smoothly the night of the concert. But Christmas concerts were unpredictable affairs—as were many social events, come to think of it.

With up to forty pupils, ages six to sixteen, you had to prepare a wide variety of acts—recitations, monologues, dialogues, drills, acrostics, and tableaux. The first act of the evening invariably starred one of the youngest pupils, assuming that he or she could get over the inevitable stage fright. One of those opening recitations is in one of my old concert books:

> *Why should folks think*
> *Because I'm so small*
> *That I can't speak*
> *Any piece at all?*
> *I can wish you Merry Christmas now*
> *And I can make*
> *A bea-u-ti-ful bow.*

The child would bow, leave the stage, and we'd be under way, we would hope.

By the night of the concert, we would have been rehearsing for almost a month. To practise in the school, we moved desks to make room for the more physical parts, such as the marching for drills, which the boys particularly enjoyed. In one school, we used the community hall for some rehearsals and for the final concert. The hall was a long narrow building, heated by an oil space heater at one end of the building. The stovepipe went the whole length of the hall, into a chimney at the far end behind a platform generously referred to as The Stage.

One year, one of the older boys went to the hall the morning of the concert to light the fire. At mid-morning, we all trooped to the hall, carrying costumes and props for a dress rehearsal. We practised, had our lunch, practised some more. Several mothers—former teachers themselves—came to help prompt the performers and prepare for the evening. Then we all went home to have supper and dress in our finery—or "titify," as one older gentleman in the community called it. (I presume it was his version of "titivate." It was the first time I actually heard the word used in regular conversation.)

When I arrived at the hall in the evening, I found the doors and windows wide open. The stove and some lengths of pipe were outdoors. The first family to arrive had found the place full of sooty smoke. The combination of oil pot burner, long stovepipe, and cold chimney had made for very poor combustion. One man said there was barely room to poke a broomstick through the soot in the stovepipe. Naturally, by the time the smoke was cleared out, the stove and pipes reassembled and the fire burning properly, the concert was quite late beginning. But after such a disastrous start, everything went well. A full house cheered on the chilly performers, who shed their outer clothing just long enough to perform their pieces. And no one of any age questioned why Santa Claus showed up in a coonskin coat. Obviously he needed it in that cold hall.

In that district, a woman who played the piano for us was a tremendous help. She not only read music, she also played by ear whatever kind of music we needed. She could even transpose music to a key that would suit the singer. I used to say that music ran out the ends of her fingers. One year, though, I had chosen a song that would benefit from a fiddle accompaniment. Our pianist remembered a fiddle in her attic, which her son had played many years

before. She thought she might be able to persuade him to play for us that night. She did and he did. We were all very pleased, as it added a touch of class to the presentation.

Later, I learned why the fiddle had been relegated to the attic. It involved another popular social event in rural Prince Edward Island in those days—parties in homes or in community halls known as "times." Before his marriage, the young man and his mother used to provide music at local "times." One of these affairs took place at the farm next to theirs. As the bee flies, the houses were separated only by a few large fields, but the lanes leading to the houses were quite long. Since it was a fine night, the two musicians decided to walk across the fields.

After the musicians had played, the mother decided to leave, as it was getting late. The son wanted to stay and party, possibly to sample the refreshments that were being shared in the barn. He and his mother agreed that she should take the fiddle home to ensure that it arrived in good shape. Instead of following the route she and her son had taken earlier, she decided to take a shortcut through the yard, around the farm buildings, and then across the fields. Since she was heading home, she would find her own field easily enough and know where to go from there.

What she didn't know was that the neighbour's manure pile, out of sight behind the barn, had a large pool draining from it, making a sizeable area of very mucky ground. The night was now very dark.

She started around the barn and walked right into the filthy mess. She began sinking. Somehow, she managed to keep the fiddle safe while she extricated herself, but how she did that I never did find out. She just didn't care to talk about it, not even with her family. When the son married and moved to his own farm, he left the fiddle behind. It ended up in the attic and stayed there until the winter we asked him to play at our Christmas concert.

At the end of that concert I thanked the fiddler for doing me the favour of playing for us. As it turned out, I was able to repay the favour sooner than I expected. As he was walking home, he slipped on some ice and broke a leg. I splinted his leg, and his hired man hauled him on a large hand-sleigh to the nearby highway, where an ambulance picked him up and took him to the hospital. It was just one more unpredictable incident in one more eventful social night in rural Prince Edward Island.

Extracurricular Activities

The second rural school in which I taught was beside a well-travelled paved road, which was the main artery from the City to the eastern end of the Island. There was little land available for the schoolyard. It wasn't really a playground. There were no such things as slides or swings, or jungle gyms—just an area in which to run around. To give a little purpose to the running, it usually developed into a ball game.

One lovely fall day during my first year there, someone missed catching the ball. It crashed through one of the windows, which all faced the road. It was the first time I had to deal with such a situation, but not the first for those pupils. They informed me that the trustees of the school had been quite annoyed in the past when they had to replace broken panes.

I told the children that if they provided the glass and putty, I would put in the window pane. (Girl Guide Handyman skills to the rescue!) The glazing points could be reused. I borrowed a putty knife from my landlord, and one afternoon when lessons were over for the day and the children were on their way home, I went outside to install the pane.

I didn't have a ladder, but, fortunately, I could reach the window from the ground. When I went outside I left the door ajar, ready to lock. Just as I finished smoothing the putty, a gust of wind slammed the door shut, and the lock clicked into place. I was stranded outside, without coat, keys, and lessons to be corrected.

At least the latch on the window was unlocked. I could raise the window, but the sill was too high for me to do a sit-straddle entry across it. Instead, I had to scrabble up and pull myself over the sill and slither down to the floor inside, all the time hoping that no one who knew me would notice the goings-on.

No such luck. By the time I had locked the window, gathered what I needed, locked the door behind me, and walked to my boarding house, a message had already arrived there. It so happened that one of the trustees had driven by the school just in time to see the teacher's hindquarters disappear over the windowsill. He phoned my landlady. "What," he wanted to know, "was going on?"

Nothing was ever said to me, and the children didn't report any harsh words said to them. I looked on the affair as just one more extracurricular duty in the life of a rural school teacher.

I had to perform another extracurricular role in that district, requiring a quite different set of skills. The local Women's Institute decided to provide singing lessons for the pupils, none of whom had had any formal singing training. It was a matter of pride for the ladies of the Women's Institute. The neighbouring school district was noted for the quantity and quality of performers who took part in the Music Festival, which was sponsored by Women's Institutes throughout the province. In fact, the school choir in the next district had taken top prize in a category for rural schools. My school was to compete against them!

A woman in our district played the organ in church, and the piano at local gatherings, but we had no singing teacher. Not daunted, the ladies went to a music teacher in the City and asked him to visit the school to decide whether he'd take on the project. He came, listened, and declined. The ladies persisted.

It so happened the man was organist and choir director for the church where I sang in the choir. He said he would teach at our school once a week if I would agree to practise with the children several times a week. If I wanted to keep the good will of the ladies of the district, I had no choice but to agree.

The school had a neat little pump organ, which wasn't in working order because mice had chewed the canvas strips that went from the foot pedals to the bellows. A bag needle and heavy twine solved that problem. Then we went to work, not only on singing, but on rhythm band lessons as well. The Institute ladies had bought drums, wood blocks, triangles, cymbals, and castanets, the idea being that learning to read the value of the various notes as they banged away would help them to develop proper rhythms for singing.

This work went on during late winter and spring. The weather wasn't always fit for the pupils to be outdoors at recess times, so we fit in music lessons whenever we could find the time—and the space to line them up. With forty pupils in one room, that wasn't easy.

We moved the organ from its corner, and turned it so I could see the children as I worked with them. I would stand on one foot and pump with the other; play the melody with one hand, direct with the other. Then the time came when we needed to get the children onto a stage, to give them some experience in a proper setting.

Our district had no community or church hall, so we had to seek permission to go to the competition and ask to use their hall, two miles away. All forty children walked to the hall, two by two—two miles there, two miles back. Three boys from one family lived two miles beyond our school, yet there was never a word of complaint.

On the day of the competition, the Institute ladies used a carpool to transport the children to Prince of Wales College in Charlottetown, where the Festival was held. The official music teacher took over my pupils and accompanied them as they sang the test piece, a folk song called "O, Dear, What Can The Matter Be?"

Our work paid off. Our school came first in its class, winning a silver cup! The Institute ladies were elated. For them, it was a sweet victory. They gave the music teacher from Charlottetown a cheque, and gave me a "thank you." After all, giving singing lessons and repairing broken windows were all in a day's work for a rural school teacher.

What's in a Name?

As far as I'm concerned, Margaret is a very special name. We have traced it back in my maternal family for at least 250 years, to Margaret Gilanders, wife of John MacBeth in Rosshire, Scotland. The family name, Gilanders, came as somewhat of an unpleasant surprise. The only other time I had seen it was in an historical novel dealing with the Highland Clearances. The mean and nasty bailiff in that story was called Gilanders. Even a name association with someone like that was a blow to family pride. At the same time, Shakespeare's depiction of a Macbeth didn't bother me at all, even though it was through the MacBeth line that the name Margaret continued for generations.

Family papers give various years for Margaret Gilanders' birth—anywhere from 1749 to 1755. My mother remembered that she had been told that Margaret Gilanders MacBeth was fifty years old when her son, Donald, was born in July 1805. Yet, according to another story, when she and Donald came to Prince Edward Island in 1837, she was eighty-eight years old. I'm not going to let the dates interfere with what we know as facts.

Margaret's husband, John, died in Scotland. Even though she had two married children, with families, living there, she decided to emigrate with her unmarried son, Donald, and two of his sisters, to the Belfast area. She was in her eighties (no matter which date of birth), and had only "the Gaelic" as her language. Of course, to true Scots, Gaelic was the language spoken in the Garden of Eden; other tongues weren't important.

Margaret headed Donald's household until he married in 1845, then helped to look after the babies that arrived until shortly before

her death at age 102. According to family stories, she was healthy enough to be looking after her grandson, Colin, born when she was 100. To say she must have been a tough old bird is quite impolite (even if true), so I'll say she must have been a strong woman, physically and mentally, to leave her home and start a new life in this land.

Margaret Gilanders was the first Margaret in the line. The second one was a daughter of Donald and Mary MacDonald MacBeth. Mary, born in Scotland in 1822, came to Belfast in 1841 with her parents, Alexander and Isabella MacDonald. Mary also came from

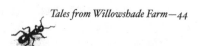

strong stock; her mother was six months pregnant with her ninth child when she landed on the Island, yet helped build the family's first house here. Mary also had nine children.

If other families were expanding like that, it was no wonder that Donald decided in 1863 that he needed more land than was available where he was in Bellevue. My mother often said she wondered why the move was to Forest Hill, but by the time she was asking the question there was no one left who could answer. The distance was about thirty-five miles across country, which may not seem far to us, but, with little land cleared, and poor roads, it was a fair way to move, especially in April and with Mary in an advanced state of pregnancy.

I presume that Donald, with help from several brothers and his older sons, had cleared some land the previous fall on the completely wooded property, and had built a cabin. When Mary made the trip from Bellevue to Forest Hill, she was eight months pregnant with her eighth child. She travelled mostly by foot over a muddy trail, with her husband, their older sons, some of their household goods, and a small flock of sheep. The family unloaded their goods at the cabin, and the male family members returned to Bellevue for the rest of their belongings and the other children. Mary and the sheep remained at Forest Hill.

What courage she must have had to stay there alone. During the night, the sheep began to make a commotion outside. Mary opened the door to try to see what was going on. The sheep rushed in, and stayed inside with her the rest of the night. When the men returned, they determined that a bear had come out of the woods, probably with a yen for a taste of this new kind of meat.

The next month, Mary gave birth to a daughter, Margaret, usually called Aunt Maggie, my grandfather's younger sister. When Aunt Maggie married, she moved to a farm in Cable Head West, about ten miles from where she was born, and worked hard, as farm wives had to do. Her two sons went to France in 1914. After the war, one moved to the United States and the other returned an amputee (Cousin Joe), and tried to carry on the work of the farm. Aunt Maggie kept a store in a corner room of her house, selling basic items as well as penny candies and tobacco. She also bought and sold blueberries, which were plentiful in her district.

My great-aunt's house had magical qualities, including a back-stairs on which we children loved to play. She also had a circular contraption on which she made heavy mittens and socks to sell to local fishermen, as well as the "stump" socks her son wore inside his tin leg. Another item of wonder was what we children called Aunt Maggie's alligator. It was an elevator or dumbwaiter, suspended beneath the floor of the pantry into the cellar. A ring in the floor and a system of counterweights and pulleys allowed a cupboard to be pulled up fairly easily. My great-aunt would put in or remove butter, eggs, cream, or meat, shut the door, and lower the dumbwaiter out of sight.

Though Aunt Maggie was not a justice of the peace, her signature was accepted as such; many a person received a pension when Aunt Maggie attested to a year of birth for someone who had never had a birth certificate. She was a person of strong religious faith, and attended the little church in Greenwich as long as she was able. In short, she was a pillar of her community. This is the second Margaret in the line—another strong lady.

Aunt Maggie's older brother, Colin, married Christina Matheson (it is sometimes given as Christy Ann). This couple's first child was a daughter they named Margaret Mary, but usually called May by family and friends. It is interesting to note that in more formal settings, she was Margaret. I knew her well. She was my Mother. She had the same courage and fortitude shown by the other Margarets. She served her community and church faithfully. While working hard to stretch Dad's salary to feed and clothe her family, she was always willing to find a place at the table for anyone who came. We were blessed by having her as our mother.

My younger sister is the next Margaret in the line, but because it was her second name, it wasn't used as a rule—unless she was naughty. Then, both names would be used. When Everett and I had a daughter, Mother's first grandchild, we gave her Margaret as her first name. In our district at that time, there were already two Margaret Howatts and two Marguerite Howatts, so we ended up using her second name, Rosanne. She in turn had two sons. In February 2003, one of them became the father of a baby girl, Nicole Margaret. I hope that, in addition to carrying on a fine name, she will one day learn about all the other Margarets in our family.

Debut at Christmas

The auditorium in the school I attended in the City covered the top floor of the main part of the school. The dusty wooden floor never had children playing on it, although I can faintly remember seeing teachers play a few games of badminton. Along three walls there were narrow floor-to-ceiling windows, which were somewhat obscured, and protected, by bleachers along two adjacent walls. This is where our singing classes were held, and this is where I made my unfortunate public speaking debut.

My performance was to take place at a Christmas concert, for once open to the public. Usually, because of the large numbers of pupils involved, an all-pupil concert wasn't feasible in the City; instead there would be little programs in each classroom with no visitors present. However, the year I was in Grade Six, someone in authority decided our school should present a Christmas Concert, open to the public. That meant mostly mothers, grandparents, and retired persons, as it was to be held in the afternoon. But Very Important People were also expected—members of the Board of Education, who placed third in our particular Holy Hierarchy, after God and the clergyman.

The pupils, filling the bleachers from bottom to top, with the Grade Tens at the top and the lower grades down below, would sing a number of selections, mostly Christmas carols. Christmas was still a religious celebration then, and religion was allowed in the schools. To fill the other spots, each class was allotted one item. My teacher decided I should do a recitation.

We were accustomed to memory work, learning poems and passages of Scripture, which we would recite on demand or reproduce on exam papers. Learning another poem wasn't much of a problem for me. The presentation was another matter, as important for my mother as for me, perhaps more so. She coached me at home. It was repeat, repeat, and repeat, until I was word-perfect.

The poem was a story told by a doll owned by a careless little girl. She had left the doll on the sill of an open upstairs window, and the doll fell to the ground below, hurting one ankle and leg, and losing one eye. The doll was outdoors all one rainy night, which made a mess of her hair and dress. In the morning, a dog came along and chewed one arm. In short, she was a bedraggled sight, with just enough strength left to tell her story.

The teacher decided that telling the story wasn't enough. The audience had to see it. I was to be dressed as that doll. The teacher provided the dress, formerly a lovely yellow silk affair, splashed with bright red and blue flowers. Some tears and patches soon changed its appearance. I was to carry a cane in my right hand, but wear a sling on my left arm, a black patch over my left eye, and a roller bandage around my injured foot and leg.

To make it easier for those in the back of the auditorium to see the individual presentations, a platform, just one step high, had been placed in front of the bleachers. For most of the acts, the pupils simply walked down from their seats on the bleachers, stepped directly onto the platform and performed their pieces. However, my teacher wanted my appearance to be a surprise, so I was taken to a room at the back of the hall to be costumed. At the appropriate time, I was let loose to limp my way between rows of seated adults to the speaking platform.

Because of the eye patch, I couldn't see very well. Besides that, the cane was more hindrance than help, and my stomach was in turmoil. But it was the bandage that really did me in.

With my one good eye, I picked my way to the platform. What I didn't see was that the end of the roller bandage had come undone and was trailing behind on the floor. As I stepped toward the centre of the platform, the bandage caught on a rough wooden edge and pulled me up short. I fell full length on my face. For a moment, I was winded. As I lay there, I heard a gasp from the audience. Then, when I sat up, the crowd began to clap. It didn't soothe my spirit. I was humiliated. I was angry. Then I thought of how my mother must feel.

So I inched my way on my bottom across the platform to pull the bandage free, fastened it as best I could around my leg, stood up, retrieved the useless cane, recited the poem, staggered to the bleachers, and sat down.

The audience, who seemed to think the whole performance had been planned, applauded loudly and long. That didn't register with me, I was so disgusted with myself. Understandably, my mother was distressed and dismayed by my fall, as she knew very well it was not intended. But the congratulations she received from audience members at the end of the concert made her feel much better. Her daughter might be an accident-prone klutz, but the audience didn't realize it.

Since then I've taken part in many speaking competitions, and spoken in public places hundreds of times. None of those appearances has been as traumatic as that public-speaking debut. It was a heck of a way to start.

Help

First Aid training came into my life when I was in Grade Eight. Our teacher that year was a licensed First Aid instructor under the St. John Ambulance Society program. She was a well-respected teacher and a strict disciplinarian, and I'm willing to bet that every pupil in that class passed the St. John Ambulance First Aid exam.

This was during a period when I thought I might like to be a nurse, and First Aid training seemed like a step in the right direction. Taking courses from the Red Cross Society, I continued up the First Aid ranks. Because I was too young to begin nursing training then, I entered the teacher-training program, and, by the time I received my first class (superior) teacher's licence, I was a licensed First Aid instructor as well.

I hardly had time to think about where to begin teaching when I was asked to substitute at a school a short distance from Charlottetown, where the teacher had become ill and needed to be replaced for the month of June. I was still living with my parents, and drove the seventeen-mile round trip on my trusty one-speed bicycle.

As a result of my work there, school trustees from an adjoining district offered me a full-time position beginning in August. It was still the custom for rural classes to begin early and take a break for potato picking in late September or early October. So there I was, after my stint as a substitute teacher, with a short time for a breather before I became a full-time teacher. I decided I'd visit relatives on the farm where I had spent most of my growing-up summers.

Bus service was good throughout the Island then, so that is how I travelled. From Charlottetown to the village nearest the farm was thirty miles. My uncle met me there, and when my visit was over he

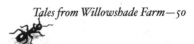

took me back to meet the bus for my return journey.

It was early evening when the bus left for Charlottetown. Among the passengers was an elderly lady who was well-known to the driver, as she used to make extended visits to various homes in the area. The bus service was very much a stop-and-go system, with customers getting on or off whenever they wished, at any place along the road.

We had travelled only about six miles when the elderly lady wanted off. The driver pulled over to the side of the road, across from the house she planned to visit. It so happened that we had stopped just before the crest of a blind hill. The driver waited, and we watched as the woman crossed the road. Up over the hill came a car. It caught her full on. She flew in the air like a ragdoll, then fell to the pavement.

It didn't take long for the passengers to get off the bus, or for me to determine there was no one there with more training in First Aid than I. So, remembering the first rules of First Aid, I took charge, assessed the woman's injuries (one broken leg, one badly bruised wrist, skin scraped off one side of the face) and went to work.

The physician in that area then was Dr. Roderick MacDonald, a legend in his own time, known fondly as Dr. Roddie. I sent someone to call him, the ambulance, and the RCMP. I asked some of the passengers to scrounge for materials for splints, and others to direct traffic until the police appeared. Some of the male passengers were wearing ties, so I used ties as bandages to tie on the splints. I didn't ask where the boards for the splints had come from, but I figure some fence lost corner bracing that evening.

Once I had splinted the woman's leg and bandaged her wrist with borrowed handkerchiefs, I placed cushions under her and coats over her to make her as comfortable as possible. When Dr. Roddie arrived, he checked the splints. He said they were fine, that he couldn't do anything more, and, besides, he had more patients to attend to. He asked me to stay until the ambulance came. Then he left.

Meanwhile, an RCMP officer had arrived, as well as another bus, sent out from town to take the rest of the passengers on their way. So the original driver, his bus, the Mountie, and I stayed with the splinted lady by the side of the road for nearly an hour. Finally, the ambulance arrived to take her and her tie-fastened splints to the hospital.

Then the bus driver took me and my suitcase to town. How strange it seemed to be the only passenger in a big rackety bus, like one pea in an oversized pod. Arriving safely back in town, I took my suitcase and made the long walk to my parents' home.

Mother and Dad were wondering why I was so late. Between bites of the lunch Mother had prepared, I started to explain what had happened. Until that moment I had been fine. Then the reaction hit: I promptly threw up all I had eaten.

That was enough to settle me down after my first real session of giving First Aid, which, as it turned out, was not as complicated as what was to come.

My next challenge occurred during my first year of teaching in a rural one-room, ten-grade school. It was a very cold February day, so frosty that hoar frost crystals settled on the scarves covering the lower parts of the children's faces. In the schoolroom, the heat—if it could be called that—came from a coal-and-wood stove in the centre of the room. The stove had a three-part, moveable metal screen that deflected heat from the nearest students, and also served as a rack on which to dry mittens and scarves. On that particular day, the stove couldn't produce enough heat to keep frost from appearing on the lower inside walls, so we moved the desks closer together than usual.

Shortly after the morning lessons began, a Grade One pupil had an asthma attack, brought on by having walked nearly two miles in the frosty air. She then threw up over her sweater and pleated wool skirt. (This was before the time of jeans for everyone.) I discreetly removed her messy clothes, wrapped her in my coat, seated her close to the stove, and gave her a little patented stomach-settling medicine. Soon she was feeling better.

The school had no well, so every morning two of the pupils would bring a bucket of water from the house next door and pour it into what was politely called the "fountain." It had to be emptied every afternoon in winter or it would freeze solid. I poured some of the day's water supply into the enamel hand basin, warmed it on the stove and washed the little girl's hands and face, then sponged off her smelly clothes and hung them on the fire screen to dry. My nose will always remember that smell—steaming clothing, combined with chalk and the ever-present dust from between the floorboards.

After things settled down, we did some lessons until morning recesstime. Despite the cold, most of the children got dressed and went outside for some playtime. Some of the boys were playing a game that involved a lot of running. Unfortunately, two of them met at a certain point head-on. By the time they reached the schoolroom with everyone calling loudly, "Teacher! Teacher!", one boy had a beauty of a black eye, the other a bump on his forehead like a small goose egg. It was my first real experience with either of these afflictions.

One thing available in good supply was ice. Wrapped in scarves, it made compresses. The two boys joined the little girl in an invalids' group near the stove. Because I was concerned about concussion, I needed to observe the two boys closely. Luckily, I had help. One good thing about teaching all grades in a rural school was that the older students could conduct classes with the younger ones when the teacher had to attend to unexpected duties.

After eating lunch, some of the children went back outdoors to play. Soon I heard another commotion: "Teacher! Teacher! We think Dorothy has broken her arm!"

O joy, O rapture unforeseen! They were right! One of the older girls had fallen and broken an upper arm. The school had no First Aid supplies, but I had my own personal kit, mostly for minor injuries. Thank goodness, it contained lots of the good old standby triangular bandages. No splints, though. I sent two of the boys to the local store to get something I could use for splints, and to phone a doctor.

The boys came back with the materials I needed and said the storekeeper would do the phoning as soon as he could get through on the rural telephone line. I splinted the broken arm, then dismissed most of the pupils. I knew when I was licked as far as trying to teach any more that day. I kept only the "walking wounded" and a few older ones to help, if needed, while we waited for the doctor. We all gathered near the stove, and I began telling stories.

Then came the crowning touch to the day. The RCMP officer who patrolled the roads in that area dropped by to give his annual safety talk. It didn't take him long to realize this was not the day for it. However, he stayed with us until the doctor came. After the doctor had checked the sick and injured and left with Dorothy for the hospital, the policeman took the two boys and the little girl to their homes. That was a great relief for me, as I had been wondering what to do with those children. I had no car, and I didn't like the idea of letting them walk home.

Once everybody had left, I tidied up the schoolroom, put desks back into some semblance of order, emptied the fountain, locked the door, and walked uphill, on a slippery clay road, the long mile to my boarding house. There was no throwing up this time—just a little crying as stress relief.

A few days later, Dorothy, the injured boys, and the little girl were back in school, and my bandages were returned. I cleaned my First Aid supplies to get them ready for next time.

Blueberry Juice?

One year when I was teaching in a one-room school in rural Prince Edward Island, a new family moved into the next district, and I acquired a small pupil and a big problem. That next community was off the main highway, with only a few working farms left, so the few school-aged children who lived there attended my school. That year, one of the farmers got a hired man with a family. The family was from the Ukraine, and none of them, except for the older daughter who worked in the city, had any English.

The child coming to school was a nine-year-old girl, the very model of a goose girl shown in pictures of European fairy tales, with beautiful flaxen braids. Sometimes they hung down. Other times they were wound in a coronet around her head, usually covered by a small kerchief. It was the first time I had ever seen fairytale hair. Added to that was the fact her earlobes were pierced, and she always wore earrings, with little blue stones, long before ear piercing became popular. She had an overload of freckles, which detracted somewhat from her looks. Even so, she was like a pheasant in a flock of pigeons.

In those days, there was no such a thing as English-as-a-second-language training for teachers, and no help from staff at the provincial Department of Education. I was on my own. So she and I coped. In arithmetic skills, she was on a par with the other children her age. But learning how to recognize and write the letters of the alphabet took lots of practising. Reading was the hardest thing to teach. I had to start her with books used by the Grade One pupils. But she was willing and eager, got along well with the others, and really enjoyed the playtimes.

The pupils who lived in her community sometimes walked to school, and sometimes rode with one of the parents. The road connecting the two districts was not a very good one; in a winter of heavy snow it was usually impossible to keep the narrow road ploughed. When it was blocked, one of the male parents would hitch a horse to a box sleigh and drive out the "winter road" across fields and through a woodlot to deliver the children to school.

At the time of this story, there was a lot of snow, so the little girl travelled by sleigh with the other three children from her area. Then came several days when she was absent. The other pupils found out that she was being kept home because she had been scalded. There had been no medical help; the family had no money and no way of getting a doctor. Thinking how isolated the child and her mother must be feeling (the father at least had contact with his employer), I decided to visit the home. I thought I might be of some help, with my First Aid skills. I visited a pharmacy, explained what I knew of the situation, and bought the medical supplies the pharmacist recommended.

After school was over for the day, carrying my supplies and lesson materials I set off on my snowshoes for the next district, and followed the track made by the horse and sleigh. The old farmhouse where the Ukranian family were living had been vacant for years and was in very poor shape. With only a wood stove in the kitchen, it was impossible to heat the whole house. The family had very little in the way of furnishings, but everything they had was crowded into the kitchen, including a big bed that took up a lot of the space. It was the crowding that had led to the accident. Table and chairs were close to the stove. When the child got up from the table one morning, she knocked a pot of boiling coffee over her shoulder, into her armpit and down her side. It must have been terribly painful.

Her mother had tried to treat the burn by applying raw egg white. Thankfully there was no infection present; that would have required a doctor's attention. Using the materials the pharmacist had recommended, I dressed the burned area in sterile bandages so that the child could wear her proper clothes again. Then she and I settled down to the lessons.

My pupil had explained to her mother who I was and what I hoped to do. The gratitude of that woman was overwhelmingly embarrassing. She kept trying to convey her thanks, and then set out to provide a lunch for me. The food was very good, something akin to bannock with fruit filling. She gave me a glass of liquid to drink with it, something like blueberry juice, or so I thought. As the lessons proceeded, I ate and drank. The mother stayed close beside me. Every time I took a drink, she topped up my glass.

I began to sweat. My stomach became queasy. I decided I'd better save face and leave before I really became sick. I could barely get my snowshoes buckled, but finally got under way, telling child and mother I'd be back in a couple of days. The cold air made me feel much better, so I went on to the home of two of the other pupils, where I had been invited to a meeting of the Women's Institute and to stay the night. The family had a good laugh at my expense. They knew the power in the "blueberry juice" I had been drinking so freely. It was a very strong wine the mother had made—much too powerful for the system of one brought up as a teetotaling Presbyterian, not to mention a youthful member of the Temperance Union.

However, I survived with no ill effects. Several days later, I went back to the Ukranian family's home, re-dressed the scalded area and worked on more lessons. The mother prepared another lunch for me. I enjoyed more bannock. Rather than risk hurting her feelings by rejecting the drink outright, I took only a few sips and this time had no problem getting my snowshoes back on. That night, I went back to my regular boarding house, and within a few days the child was back in school.

Some time later the family left the area; apparently the older daughter had found a better place for them. But I never did find out what eventually became of the flaxen-haired girl. I have one picture of all pupils in my school that year. In it she is smiling. I think she was happy in that school. I hope so.

Mayflowers and Smelts

Mayflowers and smelts are inextricably mingled in my memory. What possible link could there possibly be between the mayflower, with its dear little fragrant flowers, and slippery, slithery smelts? When I was young, there was a real connection.

One of the few places we could find mayflowers was at the City of Charlottetown pumping station on the Upper Malpeque Road—a place we simply called the Water Works. At the time, it seemed a long way from our home in the city, and in fact it was a fair walk, and none of us had bicycles. The plants never looked as fresh and green as they are supposed to. They were usually pale and matted from being buried under the snow for four to six months. It was probably the idea of a day's adventure, hunting for mayflowers rather than finding them, that made them seem so attractive. But I did like their fragrance (and still do), and hunting for mayflowers was a good way for children to keep out of mischief on a sunny Saturday when we had to devise our own recreation. So off we would go, in great anticipation. Unfortunately, we didn't often find many mayflowers, as there were usually others on a similar expedition. But we often found smelts.

A little brook ran near the Water Works, gradually finding its way across farms in West Royalty to the area of the Lower Malpeque Road, and then into the North River. Smelts made their way from the Strait into Charlottetown Harbour, up the North River, and on to the headwaters of the little brook, where they would spawn. We would find them crowded into the brook, and use whatever we had at hand to scoop them up. We were never prepared for such work, but would have a few to take home as evidence of our efforts. At that time of year, the smelts were spawning, soft and not fit to eat. Even the family cat wasn't too enthused about them. So into Dad's garden they would go.

The botanical name for mayflower, *Epigaea repens*, can be translated as "creeping upon the earth." The same description could have applied to some friends of mine who went looking for mayflowers a few years ago. At the time, I was laid up with a full leg cast as the result of a broken ankle. A woman from a district where I had taught, and who shared my love of mayflowers, decided she'd bring me some to cheer me up. She used to find them at the back of their farm, but she had recently noticed some growing in a deep roadside ditch, much closer to her home than those on the farm. She had a bad case of arthritis, but was able to persuade her husband to drive her to the spot where the mayflowers were growing. He remained in the car, and she crawled into the ditch to pick the flowers. Unfortunately, she couldn't climb back out of the ditch. She shouted until her husband heard her, and he climbed down into the ditch to help her. Then he couldn't climb back out, either. Several cars passed by, but no one paid any attention to their waving and shouting. Finally a neighbour driving by on a tractor saw the hapless pair, stopped, and helped them out.

After such an adventure nobody would have blamed them if they had forgotten the flowers. They didn't, though; they brought the mayflowers to me, along with their story. She laughed heartily as she told me the tale, but her husband, who was not a flower lover, nor as amused by the situation as she was, had a face like a storm cloud. Nevertheless, her account of "creeping upon the earth" cheered me up as much as the mayflowers did.

A feed of smelts would have cheered me up, too. Our family has always enjoyed them, but in the winter, when they seem to be most tasty, and not in mayflower season. Smelts are a small cousin of the salmon; there are marine smelts, fresh water smelts in inland rivers and landlocked lakes. Then there are ours, which live in salt water and swim into fresh water rivers and brooks to spawn. These are called "anadromous" fish, from the Greek, meaning running upwards. In this case, they are going to headwaters to spawn, usually in the spring, but sometimes as late as the summer.

My family likes smelts fried, with head and innards removed.

They refuse to consider the method my Dad preferred, which, I admit, was easier for the cook: you dipped the fish in flour, fried it whole, then grasped it by the head, pulling it free and removing the entrails in a neat little package, all in one move. This was certainly less work than the conventional method and didn't affect the taste of the fish. I can vouch for that from first-hand experience, but still can't convert husband and family to this method.

Mayflowers and smelts: food for the body, food for the spirit— and memories of springtime in days gone by.

Farming for a Living

Strawberry Time at Howatts'

When Granny and Grandpa Howatt were a young married couple, she and a neighbour decided to share the cost of buying strawberry plants. Then the neighbour found that looking after them was more than she wanted to do, so the plants became Granny's property and her responsibility. Gradually she increased the size of the planting, and began selling berries. Picked and graded, three quarts sold for 25 cents.

Then came the year of great importance to this branch of the Howatt clan. I figure it was 1929, many years before I became part of the family. One day, a woman from across the Tryon River arrived to buy berries. There were none ready, but lots to be picked. At the time, Granny and Grandpa had two young sons to care for (their daughter arrived some years later) and a small poultry business, which involved hatching eggs and raising broilers and prize-winning White Leghorn hens. With all the regular chores on a mixed farm, Granny didn't have much spare time.

The customer offered to pick the amount she had planned to buy, and to pay for the privilege. Granny told her to go ahead. That marked the birth of our U-pick business, "Strawberry Time at Howatts'," which continues to this day. Later, Granny's older son Everett (now my husband) expanded the acreage, and he and Grandpa took over more of the work associated with the strawberries.

Our years in the strawberry business have given us some amusing memories. One day, a middle-aged woman from several districts away arrived with her mother to pick berries. Because of arthritis, the mother could neither bend over nor kneel to pick the fruit. So she sat down flat on the straw path. To get to a fresh supply of berries, she bumped along the row on her bottom.

We have always made a point of telling our customers they are welcome to eat all they want while picking. That way they'll know whether they're good berries or not; we're sure they are. The older lady had been sampling some berries. Seeds got under her upper denture, so she took it out and put it in her lap. Unfortunately, she soon forgot she had done so, and in bumping along the row, she lost the denture in the straw.

The two women didn't discover the loss until they were miles away on their way home. They immediately turned around, came back to the berry field, and told Everett the story. The picking field that year was one of our largest, about eight acres. To make for easier control of picking, we had divided the field into sections from side to side and top to bottom. Because of that, Everett remembered where the women had been and was able to find the teeth.

The largest object forgotten in our fields was actually a person—another older lady, again with arthritis. She had raised a large family, for whom she had picked many berries over the years. After her husband died, she lived by herself, and since she did not drive, she had to depend on one of her adult children to drive her the twenty miles to our farm. One early morning, a very busy businessman son brought her. He didn't appear to be very happy to have to do so, and he said he'd get another family member to take her home.

Her way of picking was to lie down on her side and pull herself along the row. When noon came, she was still with us, resting on the ground, so I drove her to our house, gave her lunch, and left her asleep in our living room when I went back to the field. In the U-pick business, if berries are ripe, our work hours range from "can 'til can't," dawn until dark. Suppertime came. The old lady was still with us. We began to wonder. There was no telephone line down our road then, so it became a case of "we'd better start looking." It happened that the woman had a married daughter living some distance away on a side road near the shore.

As a non-driver who had never paid much attention to directions, the woman took some time to get us on the right road to her daughter's house. The daughter was quite surprised when she saw her mother arriving, accompanied by someone carrying a bucket of strawberries. We later found out that her son had completely forgotten he had taken her berry-picking, and that he was supposed to send someone after her. That was the last time I saw her.

Lest you get the wrong idea, I hasten to add that most of our berry pickers were quite able-bodied. When the Armed Forces Base in Summerside trained air crew, many of the families came to our farm to pick berries. One family, after obtaining permission from us, parked a travel trailer in our yard so they would be sure of getting berries early in the morning before it was time to go on duty. Some of those early-morning berries travelled far from Prince Edward Island. One day, the Summerside crew sent berries on jet planes flying north to the American Air Force Base in Thule, Greenland, and south to a base in the Caribbean. I doubt if there's much room to smuggle items aboard jet planes, but even a few would give the pilots a one-up when they presented berries "just picked a few hours ago."

In the early days of our strawberry farm, growers were few and the demand was great. That meant starting our work day early in the morning. Grandpa didn't mind getting up early. He would be in the picking field before the sun rose. Vehicles would be lined up on the Tryon Point Road, with customers waiting for the picking to begin. Whenever Grandpa could make out a red berry, we would open the gate, and the fun (?) would begin. Grandpa would leave the field whenever he wanted, but Everett and I would stay as long as there were berries available.

I didn't enjoy those very early mornings, when everything was dripping with dew. In later years, we moved opening time to the late hour of 6 A.M. with the dew still on the plants at times. Now we wait until 8 A.M. That still makes for a long day. Changing habits bring more people in the evening than previously, which usually means no early closing hours. We had a break whenever we ran out of ripe berries and closed down for a couple of days to let the berries ripen properly. It got to the point where we would say that Monday was the only sure day for picking, for we did not then, nor do we now, have picking on Sunday.

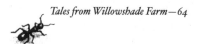

Remember the woman who lost her teeth? Her great-granddaughter brings her own children with her when she comes to pick berries for herself, and to make into jam, which she sells. Homemade strawberry jam now has become a gourmet item.

And some people still like to pick their own berries, just as they did in the days when Granny Howatt planted the first crop of strawberries. I am reminded of those early days every time I walk upstairs. On the wall is a treasured painting, done by Everett's sister. She based it on an old snapshot of Grandpa, leaning on his hoe, and Granny on her knees, weeding in the row beside him. This was the first picture taken of the planting that led to a business that has lasted more than half a century, Strawberry Time at Howatts'.

French Fries and Ketchup

What does the Spanish conquest of South America in the 1500s have in common with the great controversy over the amount of pesticide used in Prince Edward Island in 2003? The lowly potato, that's what. In a report by Jean Costellano, a conquistador, we read of a discovery at the Inca village of Sorocota: "Here at least we found their means of sustenance, a roasted nut of wonderful size and flavour buried in the ashes of the campfire."

The use of the word "least" indicates to me disappointment that he hadn't found the gold the Spaniards were seeking. Little did he know how important that "nut" would become in the lives of millions of people, influencing economies, health, and even life itself.

Samples of the edible tuber were sent to Spain, then on to Vienna where the arrival of the "little truffle" was noted on January 26, 1588. It began its slow spread throughout Europe, meeting a great deal of resistance at first. I wonder if its identification as one of the nightshade family, which has some very poisonous members, might have had something to do with the reluctance toward using the tubers as food.

The plant had begun to spread in the Americas as well, moving across to the West Indies, and on to Florida in the early 1600s. A settler in Saybrook on the Connecticut River wrote to a friend in 1636: "I hear the Bachelor is to bring us provision. I pray you forget not us when she comes from the Bermudas with potatoes for here hath been some Virginians that have taught us to plant them and I have put in practice and found it good."

As potato plantings spread in countries with lots of moisture to keep foliage damp, a major problem arose in the form of blight, a fungus that didn't bother the plants in their arid native home in the Andes. A direct outcome of the blight was the Irish Potato Famine, which caused thousands of deaths and the relocation and emigration of thousands of people.

Meanwhile, in America, another problem was spreading. When settlers worked their way westward, they took potatoes with them. Over time, plants and people met up with Colorado beetles, which had been minding their own business of living on weeds. The beetles soon developed a taste for potato leaves, and began munching their way eastward. In their native habitat, their numbers and the weeds were more or less in balance. But now, they had a feast spread before them. They began doing what any sensible beetles would do: eat and multiply.

When I was a youngster, I picked beetles and egg masses off the potatoes Dad had planted in our garden, dropped them into a can of kerosene, and then set it alight. That could still be the remedy for the bugs on a small planting, but certainly not for the thousands of acres producers grow today. In the 1930s and 1940s, my uncle used a copper-arsenic combination called Paris Green as an insecticide. It had been tried first in Paris in 1865 by being brushed on the plants with a broom. That material has disappeared from the market, as have many other insecticides. The beetles are still a problem, and as long as French fries are in such high demand, there will be debates about the wisdom of spraying potato fields.

The tomato is another plant the Spaniards introduced to Europe, from its original home in Mexico and Central America, where tomatoes were called *tomatl*. The plants are perennial in the tropics, but will not survive cold weather, so we grow them as annuals. Initially, the tomato met resistance because of its relationship and resemblance to the potato plant, whose green seed balls are poisonous. The tomato plant's botanical name, *Lycopersicum esculentum*, roughly translated as "edible wolf-peach," seems to reflect this ambivalence.

To accompany French fried potatoes, many people like ketchup (ketsup, catsup, take your choice). The chunky form of tomato sauce is salsa. In the native home of the tomato, salsa was simply a mixture of tomatoes and peppers (usually hot peppers) chopped together, used to give a little zing to the bland diet of corn and beans. This salsa was unprocessed and prepared fresh for each meal.

One year, a young Bolivian man, a participant in a Canada World Youth program, stayed with us. He prepared salsa for us the way it was done in his home, except that he made it with sweet peppers for us and very, very hot peppers for himself.

In some parts of our country, salsa is taking over from ketchup as the accompaniment to French fries, or so the salsa marketers say. For those of us who prefer a smoother sauce that sticks to the potato instead of falling off in chunks, ketchup is still the choice.

What would we do without French fries and ketchup? And how could the fast-food business survive without potatoes and tomatoes, two plants that have come from away?

Herbs—With or Without an "H"

Many plants that we now call vegetables at one time were listed as herbs. Beets, carrots, beans, peas, cabbage, and lettuce were some of many included in herbals—books about herbs—and given medicinal uses. Of course, if we stop to think about it, good food is good medicine. Nowadays, we tend to think of herbs (whether we pronounce the "h" or not) as plants that add flavour to vegetables and other dishes, in addition to their medicinal use. But some herbs still are very much at home in the vegetable garden.

We like to plant fragrant perennial herbs near the house, where we can enjoy them often, but we plant three other herbs in our vegetable field. Perennial ones wouldn't suit there, because we continually rotate the vegetable plantings. As annuals we can fit savory, dill, and basil into the scheme of a different location each year.

Savory is one I remember from earliest childhood, associated with the good smells of roast hen or turkey. It seems it is more favoured in the Atlantic Provinces than in other parts of Canada. Relatives of ours, who were born and brought up here but lived in British Columbia for years, have said that the two foods they missed most were table molasses and savory. One reason savory is popular here could be that it is easier to grow than sage, which is not terribly winter hardy unless covered by a good coat of snow.

We plant savory the latter part of May; I don't think it likes cool soil. We cut it just as the pretty little blue flowers are about to open, hang it indoors to dry, and then strip the leaves from the stems. That is one job I don't like doing, although I did it for many years. Now, just to humour me, my daughter and her family usually do it and give me a product ready for use.

Bees love the little blue flowers I mentioned. Virgil, a Roman poet who wrote books about farming, recommended planting savory around beehives. Leaving the flowers until they come into full bloom cuts down on the essential oils in the leaves, thus less flavour, so we prefer to cut savory just before it gets to the point where it will entice the bees. At harvest time, another thing to watch for is rain. A pounding rain that splashes soil on the leaves is not something I appreciate.

Savory has been used as a food flavouring for thousands of years, probably longer than sage. It was native from the eastern Mediterranean to southwestern Asia, and cultivated from the 9th century by the Italians, for it had become important in the making of salami.

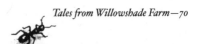

We are familiar with savory only for use in food, but the herb has had many medicinal uses. In the words of Culpeper's Herbal (© 1640), it was used "to expel wind from stomach and bowels; as an expectorant it expels tough phlegm from lungs, quickens dull spirits; juice mixed with rose oil dropped into ears eases them of noises and mixed as a poultice with flour it eases sciatica." That sounds like a lot of cures, but wait, there are more: "... it eases pain from wasp and bee stings; it is infused as a tea used to stimulate appetite or as an antiseptic gargle."

Beans, both fresh and dried, benefit from savory; my mother always put some in the crock of baked beans, and I do, too. Remember Culpeper's use "to expel wind." Let's leave it at that.

Dill is the second annual herb grown in our front field. In recent years we have grown a short, compact variety. Any dill, if it manages to drop its ripe seeds, can spread easily throughout the garden. Winter conditions don't seem to harm the seeds, and, even after the land has been worked over several times, we'll find dill among other plants. I think I use more of the foliage than the seed, particularly in potato and cabbage dishes. After harvesting dill, I freeze it to use when there is no fresh supply available.

Dill, a plant native to Europe and Asia, has been used by the Egyptians for more than 5,000 years. Its botanical name is *Anethum graveolens*. The first part of the name is Greek; the second is from Latin and means "strong-smelling," which is certainly an apt designation. One source says the word "dill" comes from an Indo-European word meaning "to blossom." Another source says dill comes from a Norse word, *dilla*, meaning "to lull or calm" and was used in gripe water to calm colicky infants. Of course, the fact that some commercial brands of gripe water had a high alcoholic content might have had something to do with calming the kiddies.

People in Biblical times knew the plant well. In fact, it must have been valuable enough to be used to pay taxes: "Woe unto you, scribes and Pharisees, hypocrites, for ye pay tithe of mint and dill and cumin, and have omitted the weightier matters of the law." The Greeks used dill as a treatment for hiccups. The Romans considered it a breath sweetener, and made it into "confits," seed and sugar cooked together, the forerunner of what we call confectionery. Nero was very fond of dill; he considered it made a man vigorous. In the Middle Ages, dill was considered to be a protection against witchcraft.

The early settlers brought dill to North America, where, in some areas, it was known as "meetin' seed," as it was given to children to chew on during long sermons. One of the old herbals mentions a condition for which it is used, but doesn't say how. Was it taken in seed form, as a syrup, or perhaps a poultice? I think that's what it would have to be to "dissolve impostumes in the fundament"—in other words, to cure a boil on the buttocks. Since dill is also supposed to strengthen the brain, I can say it goes from the top to the bottom in the (human) matter.

As an added bonus, one I very much enjoy, dill provides food for swallowtail butterfly larvae. Watching them gives me a great deal of pleasure, another variation perhaps of the lulling, calming effect of dill.

Basil is the third annual herb we grow in our front fields. The very name, "basil," raises this herb above the ordinary. The name comes from a Latin word meaning "kingly" or "royal." Basil is native to Africa and Asia, and in many countries it is associated with local religions. In India, it is sacred to the gods Vishnu and Krishna, and is imbued with such a divine essence that it is used as something on which to swear oaths, as Christians use the Bible. Basil was said to have been found growing around Christ's tomb after the Resurrection, so the Greek Orthodox use basil in preparing holy water which is placed before their church altars. Similar ideas have travelled across the Atlantic to Haiti, where basil is considered a powerful protector against spells.

It never ceases to amaze me that one type of plant can have so many uses and associations. In herbal medicine, basil has been alternately praised and cursed. Galen and Dioscorides, naturalist physicians in the early years of the 2nd century AD, held it "not fitting to be taken inwardly." Some herbalists asserted that it "damaged the internal organs and the eyes, and caused insanity, coma, and the spontaneous generation of worms, lice and scorpions." In fact, Hilarius, a 17th-century French physician, "affirms on his own knowledge of an acquaintance who by smelling it had a scorpion bred in his brain."

Despite this bad publicity, basil still became an important culinary herb, especially in Italian cooking. That may have been due, in part, to the continuing influence of the great Roman naturalist Pliny, who greatly favoured basil, especially for the relief of flatulence—an attribute validated by modern pharmacology.

Basil has an affinity for tomatoes in any form, raw or cooked. Fresh leaves are best, for the dried ones lose a great deal of their flavour. Leaves can be frozen as a purée in cubes, or packed in jars and covered with olive oil and kept indefinitely. I have tried bringing a potted plant in after a summer outdoors, but since basil is an annual, it will die, so it's best to start new seedlings to have fresh, fragrant leaves throughout the winter.

I like this herb so much that I try to keep some plants nearby summer and winter. Although I mentioned that it is one of the herbs grown in the front field, I usually grow a few plants in pots by the door or in flower beds by the back step so that I can pluck a few leaves to stick in my pocket, and take out occasionally for a sniff. Like our other favourite herbs, including savory and dill, basil gives me a great deal of pleasure—in so many ways.

Nuts to Us

Some years ago, when I was taking part in a local concert, the clergyman who was the master of ceremonies introduced me as having come from the nut farm. That brought a big laugh, of course. Most of the people there were aware of the many kinds of plants we grew on our farm, nut trees included. You will note I say nut trees, for the production of nuts, other than butternuts, has been quite limited. As trees, we have heartnut, buartnut (butternut and heartnut hybrid), shagbark hickory, horse-chestnut, and pecan, all of which Everett has started from seed. As well, we bought young trees of black walnut, butternut, and filbert.

The butternuts have been the most successful of the lot, so much so that some years I have to pull seedlings out of my flower beds. To destroy a tree is almost sacrilege in our books, but sometimes it must be done, as the bluejays and squirrels don't ask me where they may plant them. One butternut tree, animal planted, is growing in a flower bed right against an old sandstone wall. The first year it appeared, we thought we might be able to remove it to replant. Before that happened, our younger grandson removed it with the lopping shears. He thought that "Gran wouldn't want it in her garden." Case closed? Not very likely. The next year it threw up a healthy shoot. We figured the two-year-old tap root wouldn't survive transplanting, so I cut off the shoot. The same thing happened for several more years. That tree could not be discouraged. Chopping out the root would endanger the wall, and the tree is certainly growing strongly. I didn't really want it there, but we will try to keep it to a single trunk, hoping it will look ornamental—as if we had intended it to be there in the first place.

Two black walnut trees and two butternuts were the first ornamental trees we bought. One butternut had a cart dragged over it by a horse who strayed where he shouldn't; that resulted in a number of trunks, instead of the lovely one we had pictured. The second one isn't much better. They may not look like much, but over the years they have produced quantities of nuts.

Native Americans had many uses for these trees. The nuts are high in a number of minerals that "stabilize the blood and brain," according to Bradford Angier's *Field Guide to Medicinal Wild Plants*. A syrup was standard remedy for digestive upsets. That would be a medicine easy to take. We have made butternut syrup a number of years; it is similar to maple syrup, and every bit as good. The only problem is that we are not properly set up for the syrup-making job. I get tired wiping moisture off the ceiling, windows, and walls in my kitchen. It takes about forty gallons of sap to produce one gallon of syrup, just as with maple, and all that water has to boil off.

The nut is certainly edible, but very hard to crack. We've tried nut crackers of various designs. One day, Granny, then about ninety years old, and a cousin of similar age spent a whole afternoon cracking butternuts and picking out the pieces. I made a fancy nut cake with a boiled fudge-nut icing that used their whole production. I don't think I've made that cake since.

Black walnuts are a different story. The trees we planted struggled for many years. They managed to produce a few nuts, but the trees were beside the lane, and the nuts usually ended up under the wheels of a car. I could hear them crack when I was out in our shop, but that was too late. A couple of years ago, the black walnuts gave up the fight. Everett cut them down and turned them into bowls on his wood lathe.

The black walnut has the same association with the god Jupiter as the butternut—*juglans*—plus the word *regia*, meaning royal. According to the Roman naturalist Pliny, the name in the Greek language meant sluggish or motionless "from the heaviness of the head which they cause; the trees themselves, in fact, give out a poison that penetrates the brain." In folklore, the tree was reputed to ward off lightning, and nuts placed under a witch's chair would rob her of all powers to move; yet for ordinary humans, they were said to promote fertility. In the 1600s, the era of the herbalist Culpeper, the nut meat was used to treat brain disease, since it resembled a brain.

We've been growing filberts for many years, singly, in clumps, and in a hedgerow interspersed with butternuts. There is a native American species, but those we grow are of European descent and do not make good specimen shrubs. Their catkins are similar to those of the walnuts and butternuts, though shorter and appearing very early in the spring. The female flower is a tiny, red, chenille-like affair.

Filberts are also known as hazelnuts or cobnuts. The last two names are from very old English, and filbert comes from the name of a French abbot from the 7th century AD, St. Philbert. The nuts were supposed to be ripe on his feast day, August 22. That is certainly not the case on Prince Edward Island.

Though some years our filbert trees seem to produce a fair number of nuts, we rarely get to eat them. Several years ago, we had a decent crop in a hedge that's a shelter belt for our younger orchard. About the time I thought they would be ready, I suggested to Everett that he might check them out; he did, but thought they weren't quite ready. A week later, when he went to pick them, they had all disappeared. The next spring, he found a few, probably the last of some critter's cache, in the remnants of a straw stack some distance from the hedge. Bluejays, chipmunks, squirrels? Your guess is as good as mine. We'll continue to live in hope that someday there will be enough filberts for the critters, with some left over for us.

Lulubelle

Lulubelle was the name our children gave to our milk cow. We had other cattle, but it was Lulubelle who provided milk for our family for years, and she was the only one who had a name.

The cattle had belonged to Everett's father until shortly after Everett and I were married. Then Mr. Howatt (known to our family as Grandpa) decided he no longer wanted to be responsible for looking after animals. He had done so long enough, so the cattle of various ages, including Lulubelle, were brought to the barn at our place, across the road from Grandpa's.

Grandpa was noted for treating his cattle well. In winter, he carried hot water to the barn to take the chill off the drinking water, which the cattle drank from a big half-puncheon tub. Grandpa was also noted for his sense of humour. His younger brother, on the adjoining farm, employed a hired hand named Aage (pronounced oh-ga), who had come from Denmark after the First World War. He liked to visit with Grandpa and Granny after his evening chores were done.

Grandpa was still at the milking one winter evening, when through the barn window he saw the young man coming across the field. Grandpa put on his heavy woollen mittens. By the time the visitor arrived in the barn, Grandpa was milking with the mittens on, acting as if this was quite normal. The cows didn't like cold hands on their udders, he explained to Aage.

As time went on, Lulubelle was so cosseted by Grandpa and Everett, she refused to allow a female—me—to milk her. I had learned to milk during the many summers I spent on my uncle's farm. In fact, as a Girl Guide, I had received both Farm Worker and Dairy Maid

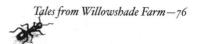

badges. I never had any problem getting a cow to co-operate—that is, until I met Lulubelle.

Lulubelle was not like my uncle's cows. Some days, Everett would be busy in the strawberry field long after the time she should have been milked. She must often have been quite uncomfortable, but no way would she "let down her milk" for me. Talk about a stubborn cow!

Grandpa had sent the cream from his herd to the butter factory in Crapaud. Everett and I decided to leave the calves on all the cows except Lulubelle. We would then breed the cows to purebred Herefords, through the artificial insemination program, to produce beef calves. As time passed, the number of animals was increasing, requiring more fields for pasture and hay. At the same time, our strawberry U-pick operation was becoming more popular, and we wanted to expand it. As a result, we gradually downsized the herd until only Lulubelle was left.

Lulubelle provided all the milk we needed, and after she freshened (had a calf) I had enough cream to make butter. We kept the milk in a metal "creamer" to allow the cream to rise to the top. Through a glass insert on the side, we could see how much cream there was as we carefully drained off the skim milk through a tap at the bottom. My mother found it both interesting and amusing that I, born and brought up in town, could make butter; whereas she, born and brought up on a farm, could not. I had, and still have, Everett's grandmother's crock churn to use. My daughter and son still remember holding on to the dasher with me and singing the "Butter Gathering" song:

> Come, butter, come. Come, butter, come. Johnny's wait-
> ing at the gate. Waiting for a buttered cake. Come, butter,
> come. Come, butter, come.

The rhythm of the song helped to keep a regular stroke on the dasher.

To produce our milk and cream, Lulubelle needed to graze in a pasture when the weather was fine. But the fences were disappearing on our farm. She was the only cow left, and the berries didn't need fences. During Lulubelle's last year with us, we would take her out in the morning, tether her where there was lots of grass, and lead her back to the barn at night for grain and water. Since we had left large areas in the berry fields as headlands and for parking, there were lots of grazing places for Lulubelle. A piece of old machinery served as a ground anchor.

One day in early fall, Everett put Lulubelle across the road in the young orchard, and tied her rope to an old truckwagon that was no longer in use. Our road wasn't paved then, and that was the day the maintainer, a large, noisy orange machine, came by to scrape the road.

At the best of times, Lulubelle was somewhat nervous. She didn't even like our little old Farmall tractor. When that road-scraping monster roared along the road beside her, she became so upset she ran as hard as she could, the truckwagon dragging behind her, along the lane toward the back orchard. About halfway there, the wagon became caught in the trees of the shelter belt and broke in two, leaving the cow attached to two wheels on an axle. By this time she was far enough away from the machine monster that she calmed down. When Everett found her, she was grazing again.

The following day, Everett decided not to take a chance on leaving her near any more road machines. Instead, he led her and her wagon parts to a place below our strawberry field, beside the peaceful, quiet Tryon River. Well, at least, it should have been quiet and peaceful. But that day a speedboat came roaring up the river from Victoria, around Birch Point. The channel comes in fairly close to our field. This time, poor Lulubelle dragged her anchor all the way through the berry field, made a right-angle turn into the vegetable field and headed for the barn. At that moment, there were customers in the yard, people who had come to buy vegetables. They were astounded to see a maddened cow racing through the vegetables, with a couple of wagon wheels bouncing behind her.

That didn't help our milk production. Neither did Lulubelle's eating habits. The last winter she lived with us, Everett did as his father had done, and hauled hot water to the barn to take the chill off her drinking water. That didn't impress Lulubelle. For five months, she drank no water, none at all. But she did enjoy eating our excess cabbages, pumpkins, and squash. She thrived on that diet; her hide absolutely glistened. There was just one problem. Her milk became unfit to drink—orange in colour with a smell like the squash juice it resembled.

Everett allowed Lulubelle to go dry, and since she was not in calf, we decided to sell her. That was probably because of an unwritten rule—never give a pet name to an animal you intend to eat. At least, it was a rule we observed. In fact, we never had meat from any animal we raised. The neighbours who bought Lulubelle for meat said the fat was pure yellow—the legacy of the squash and pumpkins.

For a long time afterward, when I would be preparing meat for our meal, my son would ask, "Is that a piece of Lulubelle, Mother?"

Respect Your Elders & Currants

At one time on this Island, many farm wives, including both of Everett's grandmothers, grew black currant bushes. By the time Everett and I started our fruit farm, there weren't many currant bushes left in our area, so we began a plot, eventually growing as much as a half-acre of bushes.

We grow black, red, and white currants. One source says they were native to Europe and western Asia, and then introduced and naturalized in North America. The generic name, *Ribes*, comes from Arabic. Another source says the currants were native from east to west, and from the Gulf of Mexico to Alaska. Wherever their origin, the fruit, particularly the black kind, has been important for hundreds of years. It is high in vitamin C and has been used as a medicine, for jams, drinks, cordials, and liqueurs. Anyone who reads about Agatha Christie's detective, Hercule Poirot, with his "little grey cells," will know that his favourite drink is cassis, a syrup of black currants.

The red and white currants may not have as much vitamin content, but they are beautiful, and seem to produce more fruit per plant than the black. The red ones hang in clusters of clear ruby-red jewels. The white ones are really a transparent golden-yellow when ripe. With the dark seeds showing through, they remind me of fish eggs about to hatch. Both red and white are good eaten raw or made into jams or jellies by themselves, or mixed with raspberries or blueberries.

Black currant juice mixed with honey was for years regarded as an infallible treatment for throat irritation. Since the 18th century, currant jam, mixed with hot water, has been used as a treatment for colds, a forerunner of today's hot Aspirin drinks. The same jam was

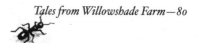

also considered an appetite pick-me-up, especially for older folk in poor health after a long winter indoors.

Because the black currant acts as an alternate host to the white pine blister rust, it is against the law to plant it in the United States. The worst problems here used to be stem borers and currant fruit flies. Pruning and spraying help to control them. Then, about ten years ago, mildew arrived on the scene. It is not easy to handle, but still we try.

In some ways, the currant patch is worth all that trouble. Hummingbirds love the bushes, which provide shelter for homes, nectar from the blossoms, and lots of little spider treats as protein snacks. It's a real privilege to watch the male birds do their dive-bombing and up-zooming runs to impress the females. Though in spring the smell of the foliage reminds me of a wet tomcat, in summer I find the smell pleasant. It's a rare day that we have time to pick anything, undisturbed, for ourselves on this farm. So I really enjoy sitting at a currant bush on a sunny quiet afternoon. I might see an osprey dive for a fish, and I certainly can sniff the good currant smell and the salt air—medicine, indeed.

We began growing elderberries strictly from curiosity. We acquired the first cuttings from the Research Station in Kentville, Nova Scotia, and planted them temporarily behind the old buildings we were trying to clean up. The plants grew so well that when we wanted to plant them permanently, it took the tractor to pull them out. We planted them in a row west of the trees separating the house yard from the field, so we could enjoy their blossoms from the house. The flat, creamy-white flower heads, almost palm-size, are quite beautiful, as are the purple-black berries. The elders had their own idea as to location: only a few shoots remain where we put them, but on the east side of the trees, there is a very healthy row. Last summer they couldn't have been more lovely.

Although we like to harvest some elderberries, usually we can't. Because the bushes are now out of daily sight, the first indication that the fruit is almost ripe is the appearance of the wax-wings, both Bohemian and Cedar. They will get most—if not all—of the fruit as soon as it is ripe.

The botanical name, *Sambucus nigra*, refers to sambuca, a harp made from the wood, and nigra, or black, the colour of the fruit—different from our two native species. Myths and legends about the elderberry, some quite contradictory, abound. One said Jesus's cross was made of elder wood, and that Judas hanged himself on a tall elder. In England, elders were planted near cottages to protect them from lightning and witches, and branches in the form of a cross were nailed over doors of barns and stables to ward off evil. In Russia, people carried a piece of elder wood in funeral processions for the same purpose; in Serbia they carried it at weddings for good luck.

For centuries, herbalists have lauded the elder's medicinal virtues. Coles, a 17th-century herbalist, wrote: "Should I give you all the virtues of the elder at large, I should much exceed the usual limits of a chapter. There is hardly a disease from the Head to the Foot but it cures, from head-ache for Ravings and Wakings down through infirmities of the Lungs to Plague, Pox, Measles and diseases of the Gutts." Another herbalist, John Evelyn, wrote: "If the medicinal properties of its leaves, bark and berries were fairly known I cannot tell what our country man could ail, for which he might not fetch a remedy from every hedge."

We might be doubtful about these statements from so long ago. But here is newspaper report from November 1996: "A slug of elderberry extract may be the best tool for disarming the influenza viruses lining up to make winter miserable. Compounds in the tiny berry literally take the sting out of the viruses by stopping them from entering human cells. Within 24 hours of downing elderberry extract, many people see their fever, muscle aches and pains and coughing subside. And even if too much is eaten, the most damage it causes is a bellyache." Now all we have to do to benefit from this amazing plant is to persuade the birds to leave some for us.

Here is a very old English recipe:

Elder Rob (Syrup)

1 quart ripe elderberries, stripped from their stalks
5 tablespoons water

Simmer slowly in covered pan over low heat. Crush
berries with a wooden spoon. Strain, pressing berries to
remove all juice. For each 2-1/2 cups juice, add 2 cups
sugar. Bring to a boil, stirring until sugar is dissolved.
Continue boiling, uncovered, for 5 to 10 minutes, until
liquid is syrupy. Remove from heat, skim. Bottle, cork,
or screw on caps. As a remedy for coughs, colds, and sore
throats, add two tablespoons of syrup to a cupful of boiling water.

Bees

They breed, they brood, instruct and educate,
And make provision for the future state.
They work their waxen lodgings in the hives
And labour honey to sustain their lives.
　　　　　　　　　　—Virgil (70-19 BC)

When Everett bought some bees in 1946 from a neighbour across the river, I don't suppose he had any idea that fifty-seven years later he would still be working with them. Nor did I realize how fascinating I would find them from the first time I watched him working the hives. The beautiful sunny day, the fragrance of the wild flowers around us, the lack of cares and responsibilities for a little time—all of this no doubt contributed to the happy memories I have of my first visit to the bee yard.

Few people realize that bees, like some other animals, need pasture where they can find food in the summer, enough to store and get them through the winter. Three weeks of fruit blossoms are not enough. There must be a continuing supply. Bees do not like potato blossoms, and since our farm is surrounded by potato fields, we must make an extra effort to provide food for our bees. We clip the headlands and our parking fields to encourage white clover. We are very happy if our neighbour has cattle doing the same in his pasture. As well, we plant buckwheat and non-modified canola.

People have been making honey with the help of bees for thousands of years. There are cave paintings from Spain, 7,000 years old, showing men using fire and smoke to help them take honey from wild bees. The Chinese and Egyptians have kept bees for at least

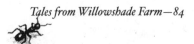

4,000 years. Egyptians used honey not only as a sweetener and in cosmetics, but also to preserve bodies in the tomb. The Egyptians kept hives on barges that were moved up and down the Nile to take advantage of the various bloom times of different crops. Present-day blueberry growers who move hives into their fields are using a similar technique, even though they are interested in pollination, not honey.

In days gone by, wax was an even more important product than honey. Beeswax candles were very much in demand, not only for light but for ceremonial uses in the Roman Catholic Church. Candles made from tallow (animal fats) didn't burn as well and were usually quite smelly. The size, weight, and quality of the candle given to the church was an indicator of the donor's standing in the community. Beeswax was used to help keep the curl in wigs (the forerunner of hair spray?), as a protective covering for paintings, a binder for pigments, and in the *cire perdue* or lost wax form of sculpture. It could also be used to pay taxes!

Bees also have contributed to celebrations of the Vikings, Saxons, Danes, and Germans, who apparently couldn't have a good time without large quantities of mead—wine made from honey and spices. Mead production led to the expression "of the first water," meaning "of the highest quality." In the days before moveable frames, the whole honeycomb had to be cut out of the hive and hung in a bag to allow the honey to drip out. Even after being squeezed, the wax would still contain some honey. This would be washed, with the resulting liquid used to make the best-quality mead, "of the first water."

There is some question as to just when the first honey bees, *Apis mellifera*, arrived in North America. Some say they came with Irish or Norwegian sailors about 800 to 900 AD. The first documented bees came to Virginia in 1622, with more being brought to New England in 1638. They followed the tide of settlement west, and have become very important as pollinators of agricultural crops, especially where that same settlement has caused the loss of habitat for natural pollinators.

At times in England, the catching of swarms was a civic duty. So important to the economy were bees that during the reign of King Alfred the Great, people were required to announce the swarming of bees by ringing the church bells, so everyone available could help in tracking down and hiving the bees.

Swarming is still a concern of beekeepers in our day. Over the years, swarms have been escaping from bee yards all around the countryside. They have set up housekeeping in trees, old barns, roofs, even between the walls of a butter factory—places where they can overwinter. Sometimes the bees live long enough to produce swarms of their own, and we get distress calls about bees appearing in places distant from us. Sometimes we can help, sometimes we can't.

One summer day, an RCMP car drove into our yard. The officer had received a call from the Department of Agriculture, which had passed on a frantic call from a family whose house had been overrun by honey bees. The family was making strawberry jam. The air was full of that wonderful smell, and, as it was a hot job, the windows were open, and had no screens. A passing swarm had landed on a tree not far from the house, and once the scout bees had tracked down the lovely smell, the invasion was on.

For a person who knows nothing about bees, and is afraid of anything that flies, one bee is too many. There were eight people of varying ages in that house, flailing arms, shouting and running around. Bees don't like that kind of activity. When we followed the policeman to the house, we found the whole family crowded into their large, older-style car, with all windows shut. The breathing of that many bodies caused the windows to steam over. All we could see were eyes peering though spaces cleared on the glass.

The family watched in amazement as Everett climbed the tree, cut off the branch bearing the swarm, brought it down

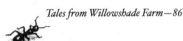

and shook the bees into the super we had brought with us. We usually like to leave the super quiet for a while so that the whole swarm will go in, but this time we put it into the back of our car, covered it with a light blanket and brought it home.

Such amazing, wonderful creatures bees are! Is it any wonder that I am still intrigued with them after so many years? The wax chandlers (sellers of wax candles in the City of London) had a special grace for the banquets of their Guild:

> *For Thy creature the Bee,*
> *The Wax and the Honey*
> *We thank Thee, O Lord.*
> *By the light of all men,*
> *Christ Jesus our King,*
> *May this food now be blessed,*
> *Amen*

And so say I, Amen.

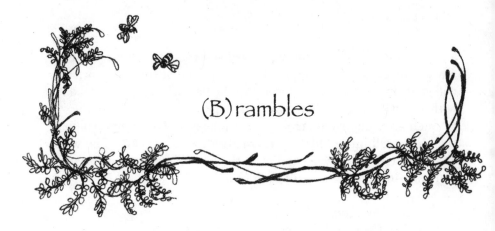

(B)rambles

As I child, I used to pick raspberries on my uncle's farm, but knew nothing about their black cousins. Until I came to live in Tryon, what I knew about blackberries came from the story of Peter Rabbit, in which the fruit was used as a treat for good little bunnies: "Floppsy, Moppsy and Cottontail had bread, and milk, and blackberries for supper." When I married and moved to Prince County, where blackberries were fairly common at one time, I discovered the joy (and pain) of picking these luscious, plump berries for our own supper. One of the first lessons I learned was to cover arms and legs when picking blackberries, and move very slowly.

My first encounter with blackberries was in an abandoned fox ranch, which seemed to be ideal habitat. Although they will grow under the same conditions as raspberries, blackberries generally produce better-quality fruit in places more open to the sun. The old ranch had good light, and the pens gave support to the canes, which tend to be quite sprawling. As well, the manure from foxes, long gone, had probably improved the soil.

The owner of the property, a courtly older gentleman, allowed all the neighbours free access, and some of us went there to pick the fruit. Later we transplanted some of the wild canes to our farm, along the headland on the north side of a field. But even under such relatively good conditions, the berries were still not very large. The canes were long and sprawling and the berries hard to pick. Like Sleeping Beauty's forest, they form a real bramble thicket with their thorn-covered, interwoven stems.

The ranch owner's married daughter, who lived in the same district, had enough of picking such small wild berries. She bought canes that produced larger fruit on strong stems that tended to be

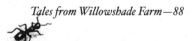

more upright in growth. She planted them in her garden, where they did well. When she offered us some canes, we were glad to accept. We planted them down the row from the wild canes. This second lot didn't do well, and we were quite disappointed.

Because of hedges we've planted at the edges of fields, the field where the blackberries are located is a real sun trap. There are times when that field is not just warm, but really hot, and I wonder if it is too much of a good thing for the berries. One reason for thinking so is that the second variety has moved itself to the opposite side of the field. I suppose I should say it has been moved, because it must have been seed from fruit carried by birds that started the new planting. Even though the roots can ramble long distances underground, and the canes can move by tip-rooting, it is highly unlikely they could make their way across a field in continuous cultivation for row crops. Their present location seems to suit them well. They are shaded from the full heat of the sun by trees to the south, yet have lots of sunlight all afternoon.

Herbalists John Gerard and Nicholas Culpeper, contemporaries in the early 1600s, had differing medical uses for blackberries. Gerard used a decoction of leaves, stems, and roots for piles, diarrhea, sore throats, and mouths. The same mixture was used to "fasten loose teeth and help eyes that hang out." Culpeper wrote that the powder of the leaves "strewed on cankers and running ulcers, wonderfully helps to heal them." That one, I think, might work. For this next one I have some doubt: "The decoction is good to break or drive forth gravel and the stone in the reins and kidneys." "Reins" is the term used for ureters. A third treatment would require a very strong faith: "The berries are a powerful remedy against the poison of the most venomous serpent."

We know blackberries, and their better-known cousins, the raspberries, as brambles, although in the Middle Ages they were called rambles. Raspberry plants are native across Europe and eastern America and have been around since prehistoric times, for seeds have been discovered in archaeological sites in Switzerland. Their botanical name, *Rubus idaeus*, reflects their colour, as well as the name Mount Ida in Greece, where they grew in abundance. Jacques Cartier found them growing in Prince Edward Island when he visited here in July 1534.

The old Herbals had a number of medicinal uses for raspberries. One maintained that "they are very grateful to the stomach, will remove tartareous concretions on the teeth and are eaten to please the taste of the sick as well as the sound." One of the more interesting uses is in the "treatment of eyes that hang out," probably a thyroid condition, and to "fasten loose teeth," which referred to teeth loosened from gums that had shrunk because of scurvy, caused by lack of vitamin C. Native Americans made an infusion of the root bark of the raspberry to treat sore eyes, and a syrup to prevent vomiting. In the present day, a raspberry extract is an ingredient in a proprietary medicine used to control the nausea of pregnancy.

Everett and I planted our first orchard with the large apple trees known as standards. Because it took some years for the trees to grow to producing size, we inter-planted some rows with raspberry canes. They fruited for a few years before being mowed down. But the roots persisted and gradually moved into the area under the trees. Some we were able to control, but in other areas they were once again allowed to grow, particularly among plum trees, where the canes really reached up. I used to joke that the best raspberries on our farm could be found eight feet up in a plum tree. Suspended there above our heads they looked like little ruby-red jewels. That orchard is completely surrounded by a spruce hedge, with beehives at one end. In summer, the orchard is so warm, cozy, and quiet, many of our customers love to go there on a sunny day to pick their own berries.

Like its (b)ramble cousin, the blackberry, the raspberry has many virtues: Beautiful to look at, a delicious treat to eat, a medicine—and, if one is careful, fun to pick.

Green Manure

When our children were small, they maintained that Everett and I had a "manure map" for a number of districts around us. Certainly we did take note of farms that had piles of what we considered gardeners' gold, especially those we knew had been lying around for several years. To see all that goodness not being used, when we knew how it would improve our vegetable fields if we had it—of course we were interested. Apart from our cats, there had not been an animal on our farm since the departure of Lulubelle the cow, so we had no source of animal manure.

Over the years we have bought quantities of manure from a number of sources. One of those was a farm where race horses were raised and trained; included in the good stuff would be pieces of bits and bridles, and syringes and rubber gloves, as well as seeds of several weeds we hadn't had and didn't need. At one time, we stockpiled some of that horse manure with topsoil and sand. We mixed it with a front-end loader, and kept it for use in the greenhouse work and on our flower beds. We still see horseshoes turning up in the mix. They make quite a racket as they go through the soil shredder.

For some years, Everett hauled many loads of hen manure from an egg farm in a neighbouring district. The hens were nervous White Leghorns, and the farmer didn't want noisy machinery nearby to upset them. That meant Everett had to fork all the manure by hand. Often the pile would be steaming hot. There's a lot of heat in fermenting hen manure—lots of smell, too. But it was a great addition to the vegetable field. Its benefits were evident for years.

We have bought many large loads of mushroom compost for that field, and now we get smaller ones as a treat for our flower gardens

and greenhouse plants. To make up for the lack of animal manures, we now use buckwheat and rape seed (canola) to provide green manure. These plants really serve a number of purposes. Sown thickly (the buckwheat particularly), they help to smother weeds and are often used to clean up a messy piece of land to prepare it for a cash crop. The plants add nutrients and much-needed humus to the soil, provide nectar for bees, and help maintain the strength of hives to keep them available for other crops that need insect pollination. We started growing both buckweed and rape seed many years ago, long before "rape" became "canola."

Buckwheat has an old and illustrious history, which has nothing to do with wheat. The name came from the Dutch words for beech seeds, *boeke weite*. Someone obviously saw a resemblance between the two seeds. Interestingly enough, the botanical name includes the word wheat. It is *Fagopyrum esculentum*, from the Greek *phago*, to eat, and *pyros*, or wheat. The second part means that it's edible. The plant's origin in Asia is reflected in the name of the species still known as Tartary buckwheat. It was introduced as a food plant, but now is considered a weed in Western Canada because the seeds are so difficult to remove from wheat. Tartary is an excellent soil conditioner. Its growth could be called rampant, but it is no good as a source of nectar, as the flowers are small and disappear almost before we notice them. However, they do set seed. We try to cut Tartary down before the seeds get a chance to spread and become a pest.

As food, Tartary's best-known form was groats, the broken grains called kasha. In some cultures, it took the place occupied by wheat and potatoes in others. We have a friend who was born in Russia, and although she lived many years in the United States, she still loves kasha. A year ago, she brought us some and told me how to prepare it. I did as instructed. I prefer potatoes.

In 16th-century England, the virtues of buckwheat were well-known. English writer Thomas Tusser wrote about it in his *500 Points of Good Husbandry*, sometimes in verse, sometimes in prose. "Brank" is his poetry word for the plant:

> *Still crop upon crop*
> *Many farmers do take*
> *And reap little profit*
> *For greediness sake.*
> *Count peason (legumes) and*
> *Brank as a comfort to land.*

It may seem strange to see the word "comfort" in that connection, but I think it is delightful. Tusser expands upon his verse by saying: "Buckwheat, which is of excellent use, if plow'd in the Blossom, is almost as good as dunging (manuring). It will grow upon dry and poor land; sowed late it cannot endure frost. It is very proper to sow it before the wheat, the ground is made clear and fine by it, and it sufficing itself with Froth (very little) leaves the solid strength for the wheat."

To provide another source of manure, as well as nectar for our bees, we began growing rapeseed. Its unloved original name came from a Latin word, *rapum*, originally meaning turnip. Many other plants, including cauliflower, broccoli, and mustards, come from this family. Now rapeseed is known as canola (Canadian oil seed).

We have been growing canola for many years, from the time it was still called "rape." In those days, Roman Catholic nuns ran a boarding convent in Kinkora, and, wearing full habit, they often came to our farm to pick berries to make jam for their boarders. Rape in full bloom is very colourful. I remember how embarrassed Grandpa was when the nuns asked him the name of that pretty plant.

The business of genetically modified canola is causing us a problem. It produces a poor-quality honey, so we have gone to some pains to acquire seed of a non-modified type and harvest enough for our own use. At one time, a farmer friend would custom-combine the crop for us, but he has since retired, and other farmers don't have the equipment required to harvest those small seeds. Consequently, for the past couple of years, we have been harvesting enough for our own use by hand, just like peasants from 500 years ago. Everett and I pull the ripe pods off the plants, and later, between other jobs, I can sit in the shade of the chestnut trees and shell and winnow the seed. We consider it important enough to do it this way, and have enough seed to plant five acres next year. To produce bloom throughout the season, and make the bees happy, we'll stagger the planting times of various pieces of land.

Canola is much hardier than buckwheat. We have seen some in bloom during a mild spell in December, with bees still visiting it. As an added bonus, marsh hawks keep an eye on it. In December 2001, I watched one afternoon as a female marsh hawk actually flew a pattern, from side to side, working up the length of the field, looking for meadow mice (voles). We often saw Hungarian partridge there as well. The canola provided both shelter and food.

Then, of course, it also provides badly needed manure—in Thomas Tusser's words, "comfort to land." What more can we ask of a plant?

Pompions, Isquontersquashes (and Others)

Those 16th-century names aren't ones you'll find listed in today's seed catalogues, but they refer to produce found in many gardens, including ours. Pumpkins and squash are two members of a large mixed family that includes cucumbers, melons, gourds, and zucchini.

Cucumbers are an important item in our market garden, both for table use and for pickle-making. To improve our chances of growing a half-decent crop, we start most of our cukes in a greenhouse, though Everett will follow up with a planting of seeds outdoors, just to be sure. As with other vine crops, they like warm weather, but problems will arise if there's also a dry spell. One of ours was an occurrence we had never heard of until a couple of years ago. It involved our friends, the crows.

There are always some crows around the farm, and generally they don't bother us. In fact, they have their part to play as scavengers. But the very dry weather of the past two years made our resident crows very thirsty. How did they find out that cucumbers are mainly water? Somehow they did, and by eating cucumbers slaked their thirst. Or maybe they just liked the taste, who knows? In parts of the rows farthest from the house, there was hardly a cuke without a piece taken out. In some cukes, the crows had left only the rind, like an empty green canoe.

Someone suggested we make water available to the crows. Everett set out dishes of water in the field, but no deal. The crows also paid no attention to a life-sized plastic owl we stuck on a pole amidst the vines. Those crows ate all the cucumbers they wanted. I have no doubt it's a habit that will be passed on to future crow generations.

One year we had a number of customers from Newfoundland, members of a group in travel trailers who spent a holiday at a campground near us. At that time, we were growing a variety of cucumbers that produced large fruit, much in demand for relish. The largest weighed five pounds. One of the men bought a dozen, total weight of 40 pounds, to take home to show his cucumber-growing neighbour, who had been trying hard to grow cucumbers, but with little success. The night the traveller returned home with the extra-large cukes, he crept over to his neighbour's garden in the dark, and set the largest fruit among the vines. Our customer made sure he was on hand the next day when the great discovery was made. What pleasure in a cucumber!

The exact origin of cucumbers and other members of this family is hard to pin down, for these plants hybridize readily. It may have been China where cucumbers were first found, but Egyptians have also grown them for thousands of years, as a food, and as an important ingredient in cosmetics. Cucumbers cleansed and toned the skin in ancient times, and still do; pictures of women, eyes covered with slices of cucumber, often appear in magazines and books promoting the use of natural products. Culpeper cited cosmetic uses—"excellent good for sunburning and freckles"—as well as medicinal ones—"for a hot stomach and hot liver, good to cleanse the urinary tract."

The Emperor Tiberius Caesar (14 to 37 AD) was ordered by his physician to eat one cucumber a day. Since his time, methods of growing cucumbers haven't improved much. Columella, a Roman garden historian described growing them in baskets of well-manured soil, in shelters of "transparent stone" (mica), from which they could be moved outdoors and inside, on wheeled platforms, as the weather dictated.

One relative of the cucumber that can be tricky to grow is the cantaloupe, which happens to be one of my favourite fruits. Columbus is credited with bringing cantaloupe to the Americas in 1492, and Cartier reported finding cantaloupes and cucumbers on his second voyage to Hochelaga (Montreal), so obviously the climate at that time suited them.

However, some years that hasn't been the case here. They like fairly rich soil, with lots of humus and moisture, and need a long

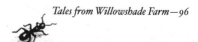

growing season. The name "cantaloupe," by the way, was applied to a type of melon developed at the papal villa of Canteluppi, Italy. Now it is used freely, often interchanged with muskmelon, for a number of types with flesh of different colours—peach, white, or green. All are delicious.

If I had to choose among the varieties of pumpkins and squash we grow, buttercup squash would win. Fairly dry, fine-textured, bright-yellow flesh makes it a favourite of many of our customers as well. Native Americans, who grew great quantities of squash, called it "isquontersquash." They would bake it and eat it whole, skin, seeds, and all. Strips dried over the fire provided a good winter food. I have oven-dried sliced and peeled buttercup squash. The dried slices made a good addition to soups, and kept well in glass jars. I enjoyed it as a chewy snack, though some of my family didn't.

We grow several types of pumpkins. It's a sign of changing times that pumpkins are now used more for decoration than for food. In years past a pumpkin was a pumpkin, general purpose. Now we grow some with long handles especially for jack-o'-lanterns, others strictly for pies (jam made from them is as tough as old shoe leather), and an old stand-by for making pumpkin preserve. Yes, there are a few people who still make it, myself included, as my husband likes it.

A friend of many years once told us about a special use for pumpkin that he encountered when he lived in a neighbouring province. At the time, making moonshine was a popular hobby. The home

brewers would remove a plug from the top of a large pumpkin, pour in the moonshine ingredients, replace the plug, and leave the mixture to ferment. When someone decreed that the product was ready, a group would gather around the pumpkin, insert straws, and suck out the liquor. In my opinion, that's a horrible way to use a pumpkin, although the drinkers no doubt thought otherwise.

The pumpkin's name comes from "pompion" in Old English, which in turn was derived from a Greek word. The Dutch grew pumpkins, too. A Dutch visitor to the Americas in 1642 wrote: "Natives have a species of this vegetable peculiar to themselves, not known to us before. It is a delightful fruit, as well to the eye on account of its fine variety of colours, as to the mouth for its agreeable taste."

Native women in those days had an ingenious way of starting pumpkin seeds. They filled bark baskets with rotten stump wood, planted the seeds, and hung the baskets over a slow fire until the seeds germinated. Like many of today's gardeners, they used bottom heat for starting plants, once again proving that there's nothing new under the sun.

Here is my recipe for pumpkin preserve:

> *Making sure to use the proper type of pumpkin, remove seeds and membranes, slice and peel it, then cut it into cubes of about one inch. Measure into a large container. For each two cups of pumpkin, add one cup of white sugar. Thinly sliced lemons and/or oranges, seeds removed, can be added as desired. (Some people prefer sliced root ginger and raisins.) Stir well and leave overnight (all sugar should be dissolved). Next day, drain the resulting liquid into a large cooking pot, boil until the syrup is reduced by half; add fruit and cook slowly until it is clear. Bottle hot.*

Creatures of the Wild

Fair Game?

During the early years of settlement in North America, the Ruffed Grouse, known by some as Native Partridge, was an important source of food. Another common name was "fool hen," because they seemed almost too tame at times. One account describes how forty grouse in a tree sat quietly while men knocked them off with sticks.

I might have trouble believing that story if it were not for what I observed. One late summer day, I was working alone in our shop when I heard some unusual sounds, which seemed to be coming from a chestnut tree close to the building. I stepped outside quietly, and there, ranged on a branch at eye level, were four grouse. They sat in the sun, murmuring to each other like small contented hens. I was amazed. I could easily have reached out and picked them off the branch. Instead, I went back inside, and watched them until they sidled off the branch and wandered away.

Another day that summer, I saw a flock—probably the same birds—walking nonchalantly in the lane. One of our cats was stalking them, but they didn't seem to be paying any attention. As much as I wanted to watch them saunter along, I went out and chased them away. It was easier to do that than to allow the cat to pounce on them—or to try to catch the cat.

Ruffed Grouse are permanent residents—no migrating for them—so we have seen them at different times of the year. One spring, they entertained us by feeding on catkins and buds of a white birch in front of our house. For several evenings we watched from an upstairs window as a bird in the tree teetered back and forth on very thin twigs, while stretching to get a quick bite.

The colours of those birds were beautiful shades of brown, fawn, white, and black. This is called "cryptic markings," with lines broken up so they blend well into the birds' usual habitat. We are always happy to hear a male announce his presence in the spring by "drumming"—beating his wings in the air.

Another "game" bird that visits our farm is the Hungarian Partridge, native to Eurasia. The grain fields and flat lands of our Canadian prairies were similar to their original homelands, so they flourished in the West. In our province, their numbers fluctuate greatly, depending on predators, weather conditions, and the availability of food year-round. Though this bird is often called the Gray Partridge, it has some pretty brown markings on its flanks and tail, and the male has a chestnut-coloured patch where breast becomes belly, which is quite colourful, especially when seen against snow. When the snow is firm, it is fun to watch them skittering across the top like wind-up toys.

The female partridge can lay as many as twenty eggs, although that doesn't guarantee there will be an increase in the numbers of birds. One year, we found an abandoned nest under a gooseberry bush. It contained twenty eggs that would never hatch.

We had a happier experience one day when Everett was mowing in the orchard. The grass was very high, and the blade was not set low. As he looked over his shoulder to see how close to the trees he was cutting, he noticed a hen partridge, sitting on her nest under an apple tree, and pulling her head down just as the blade passed over her. He stopped mowing and came to get me so I could see her. We had a good idea where she was. But her colouration gave her such good camouflage, it took a long time of standing quietly and looking carefully before we could see the movement of her dark, shiny eye.

Some partridge usually appear every winter at our feeding stations. One year, the flock varied in size every time it appeared—sometimes it was larger, sometimes smaller—and we wondered why. The mystery was solved one evening, just at dusk. Three coveys came in over the snow to meet and fight over who had rights to the food.

The partridge hop and scratch like little hens, and scoop their beaks sideways to remove the snow. They give us much pleasure in watching them any time of year.

The same can be said of the Ring-necked Pheasant, which, like the Hungarian Partridge, is a "come-from-away." The pheasant also has nested on our farm, and we are always happy when we hear the male screeching in the springtime. Once you hear that call, you never forget it. Everett likens it to the twanging of a rusty wire fence.

The female pheasant colouring is a blend of subdued browns and fawns, but a male in breeding plumage is a sight to behold—glossy green on the head, with a bright-red face patch and a white ring around his neck. His body feathers are mottled red, brown, gold, and grey. He's a real dandy.

We had the privilege of watching these birds close at hand when they visited the place where the Hungarian Partridge fed. One April, five pheasants—three hens and two males—arrived several times just at daybreak. The crowing of the males allowed no one to sleep, so we would watch them from our bedroom window. The males would stretch up on tiptoes, flap their wings and call, then eat a little, and repeat the stretch, flap, and call. It was quite a performance. The hens just ate. When the hens had enough, they would wander along the lane, with the males following them, and all would disappear through the hedge.

This was probably the same five we had seen the previous winter in the grove west of the house and back garden. Then came lots of snow, and the thick spruce hedge around the garden was completely covered. That much snow meant I was indoors, with time to watch the goings-on outside. One morning, when checking out the back garden, I noticed heads poking out of the snow on top of the hedge. Slowly, they rose like little periscopes. When our son and his dog walked past the end of the house, the heads retreated. When all was quiet again, the heads rose again. When Everett went out to get the mail, the heads disappeared again. Then there was a longer uninterrupted period, and gradually the necks, shoulders, and bodies of five pheasants appeared on top of the snow. It was wonderful to see. They lurched and staggered up the length of the hedge, then crossed the upper end, where they stopped and sunned awhile, before oozing over the top and into the trees behind.

The habitat on our farm seems to suit all three species of pheasant, grouse and partridge. Woodland, meadows, orchards and buckwheat land are all sources of food for these birds. At the same time, they have to contend with foxes, coyotes, owls, hawks, and, outside of our farm, hunters and snowmobilers. These birds need all the help we can give them. It's only fair, inasmuch as they give us so much pleasure.

Night Creatures

Until a few years ago, we had bats in our attic, never very many, just enough to know they were there. Then we had to replace the roof, right down to the rafters. The bats were dispossessed, for the new roof was so tight they couldn't get back in. Using directions from the PEI Natural History Society, Everett made a bat house, and installed it in a tree close to the house, as high as his long ladder could reach. Because of the way the bat house is built, we can't see into it, so we don't know whether the bats have accepted it, but there are still bats around. We can see them flying at dusk, particularly across the front yard, where they are silhouetted against the river and the sky. One evening when I was standing on the front steps watching them, they flew so close I could hear the sound of their wings.

Because bats are warm-blooded mammals, they must spend the winter where temperatures are above freezing, so they either migrate or hibernate. Bat houses, like the one in our tree, are only summer cottages. In Nova Scotia, bats can hibernate in abandoned mine shafts. On the Island, the more likely places are lofts of old barns or cellars of older houses, and there aren't very many of either left.

Superstitions abounded for generations as to how bats were able to avoid obstacles and catch their prey in the dark. Research has found that they emit super-sonic sounds, using echo-location to help them orient themselves, as well as catch their food. But, as Everett and I have discovered, they do sometimes run into trouble. And that is why we have ended up—twice—giving a bat a bath.

The trouble sprang from the fly stickers. Because it is impossible to keep all flies out of the building we use as our farm market, we

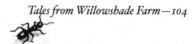

hang curly fly stickers in a couple of locations. Twice, we found a bat caught on a fly sticker. The bat may have become entangled when it went after a moth or a fly still buzzing on the sticker.

Wearing gloves, we removed the bats from the stickers, and washed the leathery wings and furry bodies with tepid water and detergent. On both occasions, the little creature flew away, seemingly unharmed. It was an interesting experience for us, although I don't imagine the bat found it so. Our daughter still gets unbelieving looks when she tells the story about bathing bats.

As for us, well, we're happy to help the bats in whatever way we can. Like the nighthawks, bats eat large numbers of mosquitoes. That makes them real friends of ours, and we're happy to have them around our farm.

Birds Rarely Seen

For years, Everett and I listened to an almost incessant bird call at night—"peent, peent"—but weren't able to identify the bird, much less see it. After hearing a recording of bird calls, we concluded that the "peenty bird," as we named it, was a Woodcock. Since then, we've had a couple of close encounters with the elusive Woodcock.

Although our farm, with its varied habitat, is home to many kinds of birds, there are some, such as the Plover, Sandpiper, and Killdeer, we can observe only from a distance. Others, such as the Woodcock and the (now uncommon) Common Snipe are rarely seen birds that we've been privileged to observe close at hand. The Woodcock is mainly a night-time feeder, because earthworms, a favourite food, are more readily available at night. It is then it does its calling, and happy are we when we hear it.

The Woodcock is about a foot long from beak to tail, with a compact body covered by feathers in mottled earth tones, so it blends well among leaves and dried grasses. Woodcock need soft moist soils in which to find food during spring migration, so they follow thawing ground northward from their winter quarters in Arkansas, Louisiana, and Mississippi, where habitat changes are having a major impact on their numbers.

The Woodcock bill is about one-fourth the size of its total body length, specialized for probing underground. When the bird feels like dining on a juicy earthworm, it can open its upper flexible mandible below-ground, grip the worm, and pull it out. A Woodcock can eat half its own weight in worms in a day. Even when probing underground, the bird can still notice what is happening around it; the eyes are set well back on the head and can scan full circle.

Occasionally Woodcocks do relax their guard, and it was one of these times that Everett and I saw one at close hand. One April day, he and I had been transplanting in our greenhouse, which is at the north end of our yard. Just in front of the greenhouse is a low sandstone wall and a flower border. As we stepped out of the greenhouse, we noticed a feathered lump in the border. A Woodcock apparently had been feeding in the soft soil and had just settled down for a rest. We stood quietly for a short time until it sensed our presence and flew off across the yard.

Another year, we watched a Woodcock probing the ground by our little pond for several days in a row. Everett had pumped out the water to clean the pond of winter twigs and trash. He let the water run onto the ground in front, which made the soil soft enough for easy digging.

Later in the season, when the ground becomes hard and dry, Woodcock will hunker down in thickets, and come out to feed on insect larvae and beetles, even seeds and berries if necessary. Their young can fly at two weeks and are as wonderfully camouflaged as the adults.

I have no quarrel with native people using Woodcock for food. Years ago someone gave me a book that included what were called "Indian recipes." Here are the directions for cooking Grouse and Woodcock: "Leave on feathers, head and guts. Pack soft mud into feathers and pack two inches all around. Bury in red coals, keep hot two hours. Roll out with stick and crack mud. Pull off mud and it takes off feathers. Take out guts in little ball. Keep feet for handles."

Included in that book was a recipe for preparing Snipe. I don't even want to think about that, as their numbers are so diminished it's been quite some time since we have heard one, let alone seen one. That sighting took place across the river. As we were driving by the end of a little-used road, we saw a Snipe walking along quietly. It was a good area for such a bird—moist meadows, boggy areas, marshes close at hand, places that provide soft mud and low cover during the breeding season.

In migration time, the Snipe likes puddly fields, wet stubble, and alder swales. What is common to all these areas is soil that has been softened by water, as these birds, too, feed by probing. The Snipe likes worms, snails, small crustaceans, and aquatic insect larvae.

The Snipe is the same length as the Woodcock, about one foot from long pointed bill to tail, but the body is quite streamlined compared to that of the woodcock, which I would call quite dumpy. Colouration in both birds is similar.

The Snipe breeds in the northern hemisphere. Those who come here winter as far south as Brazil. The female lays four eggs that are large compared with her body size. The eggs fit together in the nest, pointed ends to the centre, so her brood patch can cover them all. The brood patch is a place on the breast where feathers are scarce and the blood vessels close to the skin, allowing heat from the parent's body to keep eggs warm enough to develop.

That sighting of a Snipe was a real gift to us, one that was quite unexpected. We do, however, hope to hear the sound made as the bird dives from high up in the sky—the sound of vibrating tail feathers plus the whistling of the wind through its spread tail feathers. *Water, Prey and Game Birds of North America* called the sound a "distant, eerie sound like the sigh of a lost soul." That description is a sad one. For us, the sound of the Snipe is one that we are happy to hear.

Another marsh bird, which we have seen in our yard just once, comes from a different family from that of the Woodcock and Snipe. Seeing the American Bittern, known locally as the Marsh Hen, was another real treat. Its strange calls are not often heard, and the birds are rarely seen, probably because of habitat changes caused by farming and forestry practices that affect the marshes.

Because of the sound the Bittern makes, some people call it a "thunder pumper" or "stake driver." When I read a description of how it makes the noise, I am reminded of teenaged males preparing for a burping contest. The male bird gulps air, which distends his crop and throat, then belches forth a sound that is said to be like that of a wooden pump. When Thoreau heard its call near his retreat at Walden Pond he wrote, "The bittern pumps in the fen."

Bitterns are very fierce and will defend themselves with their sharp beak. R. Tufts in *Birds of Canada* by W. Earl Godfrey describes how an injured Bittern wounded and drove away a bull, by repeatedly jabbing the animal with its beak. Bitterns like insects, and will venture into meadows for grasshoppers, but their main diet consists of the usual marsh buffet—fish, crustaceans, frogs, and mice.

"Schlumping" through marshes is not something my joints will allow, so I consider that my husband and I were privileged to see a Bittern close by, from the windows of our house. One morning several years ago, when we were getting up, we looked out over our back garden, as is our habit. In an upper corner, we spotted a football-sized lump, covered with soggy feathers, lying quietly among the perennials. The previous night, there had been a storm, with strong winds and driving rain. The Bittern must have been blown astray from the marsh below our farm, and had taken shelter inside the garden hedge. We watched as its feathers dried out in the warming sunlight, and it began to move slowly around the garden.

The colours of the Bittern's feathers, brown, black fawny-yellow, and white, would certainly allow it to blend in among the stems and leaves of cattails and other marsh plants. When threatened, it pulls its wings close to its sides, elongates its body, and aims its long, sharply pointed beak skyward, blending in with the foliage of its natural habitat. But that camouflage didn't work in our garden. The colour of the feathers stood out, as did its long legs and long toes, which were a bright yellow-green. In the marsh the legs would resemble plant stems.

When Everett and the dog went outside and passed by on the side of the hedge away from the bird, I saw it go into the defensive pose, then gradually sink back into its football shape. Even with its head turned heavenward, the bird is able to see what is going on because its eyes are on the sides of its head, almost beside the beak hinges.

After about three hours of parading back and forth across the garden, "our" Bittern disappeared. To keep its visit in mind, I designed and embroidered a picture of one, standing among the leaves of its proper habitat. Perhaps someday I will do a Snipe or Woodcock. Perhaps.

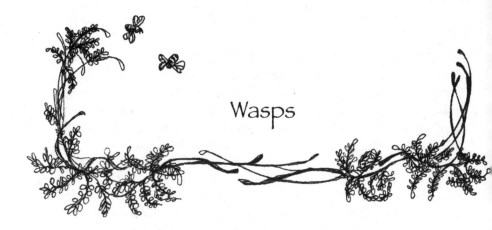

Wasps

For a few years, a large colony of wasps lived in one of our raspberry rows. We didn't mind. Even if we could have removed them, we wouldn't. Instead, we informed the berry pickers of the location, and warned them to walk around that section, even if the berries there were fatter and juicier than anywhere else in the row. The nest would have an extensive set of tunnels and chambers, and only by tearing up the row completely and disking it could it be removed.

We like wasps. They're valuable as pollinators, and their presence doesn't worry us, perhaps because we are so used to having bees around us. In fact, I find wasps quite fascinating. Their history goes back to a time before dinosaurs. Members of their family were involved in farming, pottery-making, apartment-living, air-conditioning, and the making of wood-based paper long before humans got around to these activities. Wasps play such an important part in nature, and in agriculture, I think we should pay more attention to them and give them the credit they deserve. But that does not mean I'm going to be careless. I have great respect for their stinging possibilities.

One summer, we had a nest in a strawberry field, probably not as large as the one in the raspberries. We had decided the field should be clipped after its first year of fruiting, in the hope of promoting a good second-year crop. To keep track of where rows have been picked, we use markers made of wooden lathes, sharpened and stuck into the ground. We usually try to gather them up, but always seem to miss some. I was doing the mowing and running over too many markers. The blade would clip them off, and up they'd fly. I decided I'd better gather some of them. I stopped the tractor, and stepped off—right on top of a wasp's nest. It was a nice summer morning, and I was wearing shorts. As a result, my legs were well and truly stung. By the time mid-afternoon came, when I had to sing a solo at a wedding in our church, the pain had subsided—to a substantial itch.

Grandpa Howatt had a bad experience with a black-and-white hornet that left him quite afraid of them. It was in the days when he was still working with horses. The insects seemed to be attracted to the sweaty animals; perhaps they liked a little salt, or perhaps they were just curious. In any case, the horses didn't care for the attention. Grandpa took off his hat, and waved it around to chase one big black-and-white hornet away. When the insect disappeared from sight, Grandpa clapped his hat back onto his head—right on top of the hornet, which promptly stung him on his bald pate several times, causing him terrible pain. I can understand why he didn't want one near him ever again.

One lesson to be learned from that experience is this: when approached by one of these inquisitive creatures, do not wave your arms like semaphore signals loose in a high wind. Instead, stand quietly while the insect investigates, and pray that it will fly away. If you can't manage to stand quietly, move away slowly to some kind of shelter under a bush or tree, pretending that you're an animal not in a hurry. This is what we do when bees become nosy.

The hornet that stung Grandpa belonged to one of thousands of varieties of wasps. They include the social type, who live together in large colonies, and the solitary type, who do not gather in a central nest. Members of the social type include yellow jacket wasps and bald-faced hornets. They belong to a large family, the different names simply coming from different languages. "Hornet" is from the German, and "wasp" from the Italian *vespa*. There is a small, noisy motorbike in Italy named the Vespa. I rather think the manufacturer must have had fun naming his invention.

The yellow jacket and bald-faced colonies start out with a newly mated queen. In the fall she finds a safe place to hibernate, perhaps in a pile of rocks or an abandoned mouse nest. In the spring she crawls out and looks for a suitable place to begin her nest. Once the queen finds a suitable nest, she chews some wood to turn it into pulp for the first few cells, in which she will lay worker eggs. I have one of these nests, barely one-and-a-half inches in diameter. I can only guess the queen was killed just as she had it ready for her first brood. If nothing untoward happens, this queen will look after the first batch that hatches into larvae, feeding them on chewed-up bugs, inchworm caterpillars, and other sources of protein for quick growth. The larvae then pupate and hatch into fullfledged workers. They in turn take over the job of enlarging the nest and feeding the young, while the queen concentrates on laying eggs. This goes on through the summer, with the nest constantly expanding. Later in the season, the queen will lay eggs that will hatch into drones (males) and young queens. The drones will sit around and look handsome until the young queens have enough fat cells built up in their bodies to keep them through the winter. On a fine, sunny day, the mating flight takes place. The mated queens head for winter quarters, the males die, and the cycle begins all over again.

Potter wasps and mud daubers used to be fairly common around the eaves of farm buildings. These wasps, which could be called solitary wasps, store caterpillars in their mud cells before sealing them up. It would be difficult to put a proper value on them as insect controls for some crops.

One day when I was working at our U-pick weighing table, I noticed a wasp flying slowly towards me. She seemed heavily laden, and no wonder: she was carrying a green caterpillar her own size, which she no doubt had paralyzed to immobilize it. She sat down on the table, apparently for a rest. The shelter over the table was held up by two-by-fours, and in one of the uprights there was a short narrow crack. The wasp flew up, managed to shove the caterpillar inside the crack, and, I presume, laid an egg upon it, which is what I would call real bed and board. The larva from the egg would feed on the fresh meat of the comatose caterpillar, pupate, and eventually fly out as an adult wasp. While I was paying attention to business, the female managed to seal up the crack and flew away, probably to repeat the egg-laying process somewhere else.

The nests that wasps build vary greatly in size and shape. One common species, the paper-maker wasp, build nests that are just a single layer of cells, like a plate, attached by a short stalk to a sheltered space, such as the eaves of a building, the ceiling of an open porch, or a crawl space.

People who come to our farm always seem interested in the paper nests—once we assure them the tenants have all left. We try to collect some nests in the fall, before wind and weather ruin them, or a racoon tears them apart in the hope of finding some edible leftovers inside. Rarely is that so, as the adults in the nest die off as cold weather arrives. We have nests ranging in size from one-and-a-half-inches in diameter to forty-four by forty-eight inches. The latter is a work of art. The outer layer of paper is laid on in a truly amazing series of scallops. We have others that were built completely around several apples on a branch. Another had an apple perched jauntily on the shoulder of the nest, like a corsage, with just a small depression around the base of the apple.

Adult wasps like the juice from ripe fruit. It helps the wasp if a bird takes a notion for a bite; that makes an easy opening for the wasps, and they take full advantage of it—especially since the birds choose the reddest, ripest apple, or a pear with a nice blush on its cheek. This can at times be a problem if the wasps mark up a lot of the fruit.

On the positive side, however, wasps are invaluable as pollinators, and play a vital role in agriculture. In fact, they help ensure that food is produced here and all around the world. We may not all like wasps and hornets, but we all need to appreciate them. And, of course, we need to treat them with respect.

Flying Flowers

In my early years, moths were something to be despised. The only moths we knew were those pesky clothes moths that had to be foiled by the use of smelly mothballs. The Bible didn't speak very highly of moths, either. "Lay not up for yourselves treasures on earth," it warned, "where moth and rust doth corrupt." As for butterflies, those nasty white cabbage ones that mess up cabbages and cauliflowers were almost as bad as the moths. We could forget about the cabbage butterfly for a time when we would see the beautifully coloured ones—swallowtails, skippers, admirals, and painted ladies among the many we couldn't name. It wasn't until I met up with a cecropia larva that I began to appreciate moths.

That meeting took place in one of the rural schools in which I taught. My pupils had become accustomed to bringing me creatures from the wild to be identified. Their initial offerings, a live meadow mouse and a snake, had failed to upset me. A spotted salamander had given us all a great deal of pleasure and education before we took it back to its home. Then one day the children arrived with a fat, celery-green caterpillar, about the length of my little finger, with large yellow-and-red bumps (tubercles) on its back. None of us had ever seen anything like it before. We tucked the caterpillar in a large jar with twigs, leaves of various trees, and grass, in the hope that something would be to its liking. The jar let us see it moving around slowly, getting purchase on the glass with its suction-cup-like middle feet. We watched in fascination as it spun and wove the cocoon that eventually hid the creature from our sight. That dainty silk became a dry, tough, waterproof covering, well stuck to the twigs in the bottle. During the winter, we did some research on the caterpillar and looked forward to its transformation in late spring.

Unfortunately, that did not happen. The larvae of some type of wasp had fed on the cecropia, and made their own cocoons inside the large one. It was quite a disappointment, and taught us quite a lesson.

A few years after I was married, when our children were still small, Everett found a cecropia cocoon in the orchard, brought it home, and put it in the kitchen where we could keep an eye on it. We had a lot to learn. Keeping it indoors was a mistake. The temperature in the house brought the moth out of the cocoon before the weather was fit for it outside, and the poor creature had no place to go. The next time we found a cecropia, we stuck the cocoon-bearing twig into a flower pot that we placed outside on a north window sill. No chance of early hatching there. The sill was above the kitchen sink, so we could watch as the moth emerged. We've seen other successful hatches since then, and it's always a wondrous sight.

As the moth emerges, it seems such a weak, soggy creature, with wings like wet tissue paper tight to its sides, and bearing little resemblance to the beautiful creature it will become. The hatch is a slow process. Fluids from the body are gradually pumped into the wing, which unfold and begin to expand. The body shrinks in length, and colours darken. It is amazing to think that everything necessary to produce a large moth, whose wings spread as wide as my hand, is in that slowly pulsing body. At one point, I saw it lift its lower body up towards its chest (thorax) then down, almost like a human doing leg lifts. In this case, the cecropia was using its own abdomen as a pump to get fluids into the expanding wings. Then it began to exercise the wings, slowly and gently lifting and lowering. After several hours. the wings were expanded enough. Then the moth began moving the front pair in a figure-eight, like the sculling pattern we are taught for treading water. The back wings just lifted and lowered, lifted and lowered.

This business began in early morning. By 9 A.M., the moth was out of the cocoon. By 7 P.M., the work was completed, and it was resting on the twig where it had spent the winter. The body was now short, thick, and beautifully marked with bands of cinnamon and white, shoulders almost orange and the rest of the body a furry, dark brown. The wings were bordered with bands in varying shades of fawn and brown, each one with a large eye spot, light with a dark band.

The moth I'm describing so minutely was one I made a point of observing carefully. Several times through that day, visitors watched the process with us, and my son took pictures. The moth was still on the twig at 9 P.M. An hour later, I went outside with a flashlight to check again. It was gone.

Because of this moth's fern-like (plumose) antennae, I am fairly sure it was a male. The antennae act as receptors for the phero-mones released by female moths. The mouth parts of a moth are quite reduced, and they do not feed, so the life of a fullfledged moth is rather short. Seeking a mate is its only reason for being. The ce-cropia moths are nocturnal flyers, so not often seen. We have been fortunate to have seen these beautiful creatures go through such amazing life stages.

The name, cecropia, came from a Greek myth in which the first ruler of Athens was a half-human, half-dragon, named Cycrops. An-other moth, the polyphemus, similar to cecropia, also obtained its name from Greek mythology, and is also a silk moth and night flyer. Because of its large size and eye-spots (large on hind wings, smaller on front ones), it was named after the one-eyed giant who had im-prisoned Ulysses and his friends, but was eventually tricked into freeing them. The larva is about the same size and colour as that of the cecropia, but with more knobs. The cocoons of the polyphemus are usually found much lower than those of the cecropia—even on the ground sometimes, or attached by one end to a twig, whereas the cecropia is attached along its whole length.

One spring evening, we found our youngest cat playing with a polyphemus moth on the floor of the porch. We were surprised to see it there, and figured the cocoon must have been on plants or pots we had taken back into the flower room at the end of a summer out-of-doors. Because of the heat indoors, the moth had hatched before its proper time. The eye spots on the hind wings of this moth were very striking, almost like little mirrors, and would certainly deflect a hungry bird from the plump body. The markings, with banding on the wings, were similar to those of a cecropia, although the colours were more muted. We put the polyphemus in a hanging pot in the flower room for the night, but couldn't find it the next day. It may have fluttered back to the floor, where the cat dispatched it. We accepted that fate only by telling ourselves it couldn't have survived outdoors anyway. We were grateful that we had the chance to see such a rare silk moth.

Even though swallowtail butterflies are fairly common around our gardens, we appreciate them, too, and love to watch them in their larval stage. We grow dill for customers who want it for pickle-making, and there is usually enough to feed the larvae of the black swallowtail as well. At a certain time in the summer, we can be sure of finding some of these fat, strikingly coloured larvae on the dill; they have black-and-green bands with yellow spots on the black. If the larvae are disturbed, two little horns appear on the head. They look like tiny orange-red pipe cleaners, and are designed to scare off anything looking for a juicy meal. Once the larvae reach a certain size, they disappear. I find it quite amazing: one day they are there, munching away; the next they are gone, and where they go to pupate, I don't know. We just hope there will be more another year.

Painted ladies, or vanessas, as they are sometimes called, appear when the perennial asters are in bloom in September. That was when we saw our one and only monarch. We were able to verify it because a youth group was visiting the farm that day, and their leader photographed the monarch. We often see admirals and mourning cloaks, and sometimes cinnabar moths, with their striking red markings.

I realize that the larvae of some of these beautifully coloured moths and butterflies may cause damage to plants that people treasure, but the ones we see here are so few, and usually feed on such a variety of plants, that we can continue to enjoy these creatures and to marvel at the way nature has formed these "flying flowers."

Dark Meat or White?

For many years, the Goose Supper used to be the most important social event of the fall in Prince Edward Island, particularly in rural areas. Once the crops were all under cover, and the ploughing for next year's planting was under control, then came the time for celebration. Many farm families had flocks of geese, enough for the needs of the owner, and perhaps a few to sell for some scarce cash.

"Christmas is coming; the goose is getting fat." So goes a line from an old round song. A goose was associated with the Christmas feast long before turkeys became even available, let alone popular. The reason was very simple: geese were much easier—and less costly—to raise than turkeys.

It wasn't only for meat that geese were prized. In ancient Rome, they served as watchdogs. At one time in Wales, it was common to leave a hole under the steps into the house where a goose could stay at night and warn of any intruder. An angry, hissing goose is a scary sight, and has great power for harm in its wings. In the present day, some distilleries in Scotland keep flocks of geese on patrol to ensure that casks of maturing whiskies are undisturbed.

Geese have also provided a myriad of useful products. Goose grease as a chest rub was still in use when I was a youngster. Rubbed in well, covered by a warm piece of wool flannel, goose grease would give some comfort; I'm not sure about cure. Of course, it wasn't only on chests that the grease was used. It never hardened, so was much in demand as a lubricant, especially on dairy and milling equipment. Goose grease also came in handy for waterproofing leather boots. My Dad had a pair of heavy, knee-high leather Wellington boots for which he would heat up an odd-smelling mixture, to be applied with a brush. He said it would keep the boots supple as well as waterproof. What I chiefly remember about those boots was the need of a bootjack to remove them; no child's hands could pull them off Dad's feet.

In the days of the knights, goose grease kept their armour from rusting, and served the same function on the kitchen spit that held their roasting meat. Goose grease could also make up for any lack of lanolin in a wool fleece. If the lanolin that kept the wool soft was removed in the wash, goose grease could be added during the combing process to help prevent the fibres from breaking on the spinning wheel.

Goose feathers had many uses, and still do. I like goose-wing dusters, and am fortunate to have a friend who can keep me supplied with the wings. I treat them as my grandmother did, by sticking the bony ends in coarse salt to cure them, then wrapping them in fabric to make a hand grip. The salt curing prevents buffalo bugs (larder beetles) from infesting them.

Duvets are much more fashionable now than what we used to call "puffs" or "comforters"—coverings filled with cotton or wool batting. But feather duvets are not new (*duvet* is a French word that meant a fine, downy feather). They have been a part of households for hundreds of years. Consider winter nights in houses where the only heat was from fireplaces, and you will understand why feather beds and covers were so important. I remember sleeping in, not on, a feather bed at a great-aunt's house. I can understand what a comfort such a bed would be when winter winds howled.

At one time, goose-feather beds helped keep sailors comfortable on board and afloat overboard. According to *Lost Country Life* by Dorothy Hartley, a 14th-century practice was to make a cover of heavy linen, stuff it with feathers, waterproof it with beeswax, and tie off the corners so they could be used as handles. On little coastal vessels, this affair would serve as a mattress, laid on top of whatever cargo the sailors were carrying, and as a life raft if the ship sank. The buoyancy of the feathers, inside the waxed cover, made the little raft almost unsinkable. Such a use was noted in the "Ballad of Sir Patrick Spens" from the 13th to 14th century. This was a story of a trip in stormy weather between Scotland and Norway, with sad results:

O mony was the feather bed
That floated on the foam,
Mony were gude lord's sons
That never mair came home.

In days gone by, quills from goose feathers had all kinds of roles: pens (think of penknives), stoppers in bottles, spigots in casks, teats in bottles to feed human or animal babies. Nowadays we often see quills with ball points, used for signing guest books at fashionable affairs.

With so many varied uses in the past, it is no wonder that a flock of geese was considered an asset on a farm, especially when their food consisted mostly of grasses.

Some Islanders still raise geese, mostly as birds for exhibition, but turkeys have taken over as the centre of the Christmas feast. Long before Europeans came to the Americas, the Aztecs of Mexico had domesticated a gobbling, strutting fowl, the largest of the game birds. Their name for it was *uexcolotol*—pronounce that if you dare. Natives in northern forests hunted the creature with bow and arrow, but these birds were wily prey, a far cry from the ones we buy now. About 1520, Spaniards took turkeys to Europe and began raising and exporting them. Because Turkish trading vessels carried the birds to England when they first appeared on the royal table of Henry VIII in 1540, they were called "turkey fowle," and the name stuck.

When Everett was a youngster, a farmer next to his cousin's farm kept turkeys. They became quite a nuisance to members of his cousin's family, roosting in their fruit trees at night, and waking them rudely early in the morning with their gobbling and squawking. The turkeys probably sampled the fruit, too. Finally the owner was warned the birds would be shot if they weren't kept home. They were.

At one time I boarded on a farm where turkeys were raised commercially. I learned how difficult the poults are to raise without the care of a mother turkey. They sometimes needed help in learning how to eat and drink, and they didn't have sense enough to get in out of the rain. I remember family members rushing to get them indoors out of a rain shower before they became chilled.

The grandfather of that family took charge of cooking the turkey for family feasts. To ensure a lovely, moist bird he covered it in cheesecloth dipped in melted butter. The result was always good—very good.

In other parts of the world, the dressing (or stuffing) for the bird often reflected the diet of the area. It's no surprise, then, that in Spain the main ingredient was olives, and in France, chestnuts, sometimes just chopped and other times as a paste with bread, eggs, cream, and herbs. Apparently the turkeys of days gone by didn't have much fat on them; recipes often included pork fat or fat meat in the ingredients. The recipe that the chef to Napoleon's chancellor concocted is the one that really takes the prize. He would stuff a Turkey with a Capon, the Capon with a Partridge, the Partridge with a Quail, the Quail with an Ortolan (a small bird similar to a bunting), and the Ortolan with an olive. One account of this culinary delight remarks that "only the olive was eaten." That may have been the case in the high-society dining room, but I'll bet the kitchen help soon devoured the rest.

In many present-day recipes, sage is the herb of choice for turkey dressing, although Maritimers seem to prefer savory. In our household, dressing made with bread, mashed potatoes, onions, savory, salt, and pepper makes a turkey a dish fit for anyone—king, chancellor, or hard-working farmer!

Owls

When an elderly relative gave us some family papers a few years ago, we found a sheet showing the Howatt clan crest. We were delighted to see three owls prominently displayed, for we've always considered owls fascinating birds.

Owls are a part of the wildlife on our farm, the great horned owl being the one we hear most. It usually starts calling in February and continues into the summer. Even though we consider owls to be creatures of the night, we can hear this one booming its five-note call most often in the daytime.

The Horned Owl's diet is quite varied. For the one or more owls living near us, there are woodlands, open fields, orchards, and marshy shores to provide a large menu. As an example of the owl's eclectic tastes, an American ornithologist, Charles Bendire, wrote of a nest that contained "a mouse, a young muskrat, two eels, four bullheads (a type of catfish), a woodcock, four ruffed grouse, one rabbit and 11 rats." We don't have catfish in this area, but we can supply all the other items on the owl's grocery list.

The Great Horned Owl is one of the few creatures that will tackle a skunk. We wonder whether that trait accounts for the loss of one of our cats. Our family remembers the occasion well. My parents, visiting us one summer, were having trouble sleeping at night because of the booming call of one of these birds. For about a week during the full moon, it had taken up station on a birch tree sixty feet away from their bedroom. Though I can't remember the exact words Dad used, I know he had a lot to say about "that owl."

At the time, we had a young male cat, mostly black but with enough white markings to make him resemble a skunk, especially from a distance, moreso at night time. The cat disappeared one night during the owl's visit. Did the cat become an out-of-the-ordinary treat for that owl?

Another owl in this area, one we see on an irregular basis, is the Snowy Owl. We don't usually expect to see one until late winter, when a shortage of food in its northern home tends to bring the birds south. But in the year 2002, a Snowy Owl was spotted in early January in a field at the end of the Tryon Point Road, perched on top of a mound of earth. A little elevation no doubt helps in sighting prey. We have seen one owl using a fence post as a lookout.

I first encountered a Snowy Owl when I was in my early teens. I have a picture from that time of Dad and myself, holding up a dead owl, wings extended, to show its full size. Dad had found it on one of the firing mounds on the Rifle Range at Alexandra Point. He would have liked to have had it mounted, but dollars were too scarce for such things.

I had a close encounter of a much more lively owl one evening in early spring, when I was walking to choir practice in our local church. It was just before full dark, and up ahead I could see a large form quartering back and forth across a field, as hawks do when hunting. After the bird had made three or four passes, I lost sight of it. Suddenly, from the edge of the field beside me, a Snowy Owl rose up and flew away, leaving me quite startled for a minute by the side of the road.

A few years ago, a young man from Victoria found an injured Snowy Owl in a field, took it home, and gave it free run in his house. In the spring, the healed owl travelled back north by airplane. My son had taken pictures of the bird, and I eventually did a large needlepoint portrait, which is now in our son's living room.

Both the Horned Owl and the Snowy Owl are large birds, up to two feet in length. The Saw-whet Owl, on the other hand, is only about seven to eight-and-a-half inches, hardly as big as a Robin, and is rarely seen around here. One April evening, Everett and I were about ready for bed when we heard the sound of tapping on metal, coming, we thought, from our neighbour's farm just up the road. Our neighbour has a well-equipped workshop where he does repairs to his farm machinery, and he's noted for working late at night.

This was not a full, clanging-on-anvil sound, but a light tap with a bit of a drag. We went to bed and forgot about it until the next night when the noise began again. This time we opened the back door overlooking our perennial garden, and were able to determine the sound was coming from the trees behind the garden hedge. Everett went out in the dark and walked around until he isolated the tree he thought the sound was coming from. Then, by listening to some bird-song records, we concluded that a Saw-whet Owl was in the neighbourhood. The next day, Everett went back to the tree but could see no sign of the bird. The owl repeated its call a third night. After that, we didn't hear it again. It must have moved on after receiving no response to its message.

At least, that short visit has allowed us to claim association with three species of owls—quite appropriate, I think, for a family with a crest bearing three owls. By the way, the family motto on that crest is *Post Tenebras Lux*, meaning "After Darkness Light." It would be nice to have an explanation for the motto—and for the owls.

Eagles and Ospreys

Our family is continually grateful for the wisdom of the ancestors who, over two hundred years ago, chose this piece of land on which to settle. Its location brings us benefits far beyond the value of the food we produce. We are on a point of land with the Tryon River on the east, Northumberland Strait to the south, and Cumberland Cove west, bodies of water providing lots of room for birds that like to fish.

The river is the fishing ground for both Ospreys and Bald Eagles; with their numbers on the increase, we expect to see them through the summer when we are out working in our fields. One benefit of having to hoe berry plants (we don't use herbicides on them) is being able to keep an eye on activity over the water, something not easy to do when driving a tractor.

Osprey numbers had been in sharp decline because of the use of DDT; since it was banned the birds are having much better luck in raising their young. Once the ice is out of the river, we will listen for their calls, which tell us they are back from their wintering grounds. Large birds—brown-black, with mostly white underparts and swept-back wings—they are a wonderful sight as they glide, then hover, glide and hover again; with their excellent eyesight allowing them to see a fish from fifty feet above the water.

So adept at hovering are the Ospreys that we say they are "sitting on the wind." Then comes the swift dive, and with luck there will be a fish in the talons of the specialized feet. The outer toes aren't fixed, but can move forward and back, and there are spiny processes for holding on to slippery fish. Anyone who has lost his hold on a wiggling fish could appreciate having "grippers" to hang on to it.

We have seen an Osprey nest on the bank of the next river to the east, but don't know exactly where "ours" have set up housekeeping. It can't be too far away, for the parents bring their young here for flight training. In late July/early August, they will start exercising their legs with knee-bends and stretches, and their wings by a great deal of flapping. One windy August day I watched a family of four fly over the river that lies at the bottom of the field behind our shop. The two young ones were having difficulty getting the right angle on their wings because of the gusty winds. They would take a breather on some tall trees along the bank, then try again.

The Bald Eagle is misnamed because the adult's head is fully covered by white feathers. Someone wrongfully interpreted an old European word that meant having a white spot. That white head may help the crows that zero in on the Eagles, who suffer from the same harassment as the Ospreys. Young eagles' head feathers are brown; it takes from four to seven years before the white feathers of an adult appear. The body feathers on all ages are the same dark brown, which, from a distance, appears black.

For thousands of years the Eagle has been the symbol of might and power. It went into battle with the early Persians. Its likeness topped the standards of mighty Roman legions and went before them on their conquest of other lands. In the present day, the symbol has been appropriated by the country south of us; it appears on their money, their government documents, and presidential seal. Parallels in history.

The Eagle has several ways of getting dinner. It may catch its own, or it may lie in wait until an Osprey has something in its talons. Then the Eagle will pester the Osprey until it drops the fish, then swoop in and pick the catch out of the air. It hardly seems fair to the Osprey, but that's the way it is.

I think the Eagles are inquisitive. On different ccasions we have been out working in our fields with, each time, three Eagles soaring around and around above us. Of course, on a lovely summer day it must have been quite pleasant where they were—rising thermals giving lift without much expenditure of effort on their part. I usually get a crick in my neck or back from trying to watch them watching us.

One summer day, our grandson Jeremy was on duty at the weighing table in the strawberry field. An adult eagle flew in and sat on a tree behind him for some time before flying along the trees down to the river. In the early fall of 2001, Everett watched one on the mud flats across the river. Its feet appeared to be caught in something, and it struggled quite a while before freeing itself.

We should carry binoculars with us the whole time. One day when Everett and I were both in the shop, we saw an Eagle on the top of a tall spruce, on the edge of our farthest field, so Everett went to the house for binoculars. If the Eagle had been in its usual place, we wouldn't have needed them. We checked on the bird periodically, and it stayed for about an hour.

A clergyman friend of ours had a Scripture verse he used often: "They that wait upon the Lord shall renew their strength, they shall rise up on wings like eagles, they shall run and not be weary, they shall walk and not faint." During a bout with cancer, I repeated those words a lot. There is a version set to music, which I hum or sing to myself, "And I will raise you up on eagle's wings, bear you on the breath of dawn, make you to shine like the sun, and hold you in the palm of my hand."

These are wonderful images to hold in the mind when out hoeing on a hot, muggy, mosquitoey day—or any day—helped along by the sight of Eagles and Ospreys.

Cousins Under the Fur

One summer evening, when Everett and I were hoeing in the field by the river, we decided to relax on the bank for a few minutes. Along came a skunk family: mother and four cute kits following behind in single file. We sat very still. They passed behind us, about two feet away. They were chittering and squeaking as they went, minding their own business and paying no attention to us. Skunks' eyesight is poor, so to them we may have just been two unmoving blobs that were no cause for concern.

As long as they adopted that attitude, they didn't worry us, either. Neither the skunk nor its cousin, the weasel—otherwise known by the more elegant name, ermine—poses any threat to our present way of farming. In fact, we're quite happy to see them on our farm. But both animals were hated in the days when many farms relied on a flock of hens to provide much appreciated egg money.

Grandpa Howatt's hens were important not only as egg producers but as the basis of his hatchery business. His White Leghorns were top-quality, and he looked after them well. Before he settled down for the night, he would check to see that all was well in the henhouse. White Leghorns are very nervous, and Grandpa always knocked on the henhouse door before entering so as not to startle them. One evening, when the hens should all have been on the roost, he saw a movement in one of the nest boxes. It was almost dark. Grandpa thought there might be a skunk in the box. He got his shotgun and fired away. Alas, when things settled down he found he had shot one of his prize hens.

When it comes to diet, skunks are omnivorous. They like rats, mice, snakes, grasshoppers, eggs, young birds, and larvae of many kinds. We are glad they like June bug larvae. Many people become

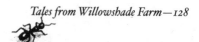

annoyed when they see the holes foraging skunks have dug in their lawns. What the lawn-owners don't realize is that the skunks are doing them a favour.

In addition to their carnivorous diet, skunks also like bird seed and sweet corn. Blue jays, when fighting at the bird feeders, always manage to spill some seed, and what the ground-feeding birds won't eat, the skunks will. When it comes to corn, skunks are not as destructive as raccoons, which mess up much more than they eat. A skunk will completely clean off a cob. Everett watched one that sat on its haunches, reached up and pulled an ear off with its front paws, then stripped off the husks and proceeded to enjoy a feast of fresh corn. Skunks have a sweet tooth, too. They will wait beside a hive to catch returning bees loaded with nectar. Their fur is too thick for bees to penetrate, and a few jabs on the face don't seem to bother them. There are times when they do some scratching around the hives, but they haven't been a real problem for us, as they have been in other parts of Canada.

You can expect to see skunks at any time, anywhere in the province, from March to December. Skunks were not native to Prince Edward Island, but arrived at the time of the silver fox boom, when someone thought to cash in on the demand for fancy furs. In the early 1900s, skunks were brought in to be ranched in the same way foxes were. The skunks didn't have the foxes' long, silver guard hairs, but the skunks' black-and-white coats actually wore better. When the bottom dropped out of the fur market, skunks were not worth even the cost of their feed, so they were released and quickly made themselves at home.

The scientific name of this pretty, smelly creature is *Mephitis mephitis*; the one word used twice seems to reinforce the meaning, "a noxious or pestilential exhalation from the ground." The word is related to "Mephistopheles," which certainly conjures up pictures of something nasty. Yet, at the same time, the perfume industry uses the very powerful skunk oil as a fixative for some products. A skunk, fully loaded, has enough ammunition for four to six discharges, which can be propelled as far as fifteen feet. The young ones have fire power at two months of age.

Weasels, which are native to the Island, have about the same taste in food as their skunk cousins—rats, mice, birds, frogs, rabbits, carrion. They will climb shrubs to find birds' nests or even take to water to catch a duckling. A weasel feeds any time of the day or night, and may stop for a rest in the burrow or den of a creature it has just eaten. Ounce for ounce, the weasel is about the most bloodthirsty of creatures; it will fight animals many times its size and often wins.

In summer, the species on the Island, the short-tailed weasel, is mostly brown, with a darker tip on the tail. With the shorter days of autumn, the pituitary glands cause hormonal changes that result in a snowy white winter coat, with the dark tail tip really showing up. It was the winter pelt, known as ermine, that at one time was reserved by law for royalty, the lordly classes, and the judiciary (who at one time were Lords). Now the pelts go to the highest bidder.

Like the skunk, the weasel can be a pest. A neighbour of ours has been raising heavy meat-breed hens for a few years to supply her own needs and those of a fortunate few customers. Those birds were really choice eating. A weasel must have thought so, too. One got into the henhouse when the birds were only half-grown, and killed a large number of them. That meant no meat for those outside the household. On other farms, though, the weasel can be a friend, helping to keep rats and mice under control.

Unlike the skunks, weasels are elusive and rarely seen. I consider myself fortunate to have seen a weasel at close quarters on two different occasions, both in July, from my weighing table set up in the field at strawberry-picking time. The first visit from a weasel took place in the field next to our main orchard. I noticed a little animal come out of a swampy area and hurry along the lane at the bottom of the field. Instead of continuing on the track, it veered off, walked right under the bench on which I was sitting, then scurried over the headland and into the orchard.

The second sighting was again in a strawberry field by the shore, where a small section of marsh probably would provide a few treats for a weasel. I was at my usual post, the weighing table, and the pickers were on the far side of the field. Up from the shore, along the headland, came a weasel, hurrying along. It passed close to my feet and disappeared into the long grass behind me. I could almost hear it muttering, like the White Rabbit in *Alice In Wonderland*, "I'm late, I'm late!"

With their ammunition, skunks have adjusted quite well to living among humans, and unless a disease such as rabies hits them, they probably will continue to do so. Its little cousin with the coveted fur, *Mustela ermina*, the weasel, is having a difficult time where clearcutting and monoculture are removing suitable habitat. In the meantime, we hope conditions on our farm will continue to be to its liking.

Signs of Spring

The calendar may say that spring arrives with the Equinox in March, but for many of us Islanders, it comes with the first sound of Canada Geese. They may have to stay off-shore for a time before the ice leaves the rivers and bays, but there are always a hardy few to act as the vanguard of the flocks we expect later. We are fortunate to live on the Atlantic flyway, which gives us a front-row seat for the waterfowl migration, the Tryon River being one of their prime staging areas.

Once the ice is gone, the geese make themselves quite at home in the river—great rafts of them moving back and forth. For a change from eel grass and other seaweeds, they fly into the fields to feed and fatten up before heading farther north to their nesting grounds. A few birds nest on the Island. They will have grain (sometimes lots of it) left behind by the combines, as well as clovers that have over-wintered. Some say geese harm the clover, while others say they just nip off the leaves, and leave the crown to "stool" (spread) out. The geese also eat potatoes—frozen or not—that were small enough to fall through the chains on the digger.

Our farm offers the geese a varied menu. They come up from the river and root through the straw covering our berry plants. One year we had about a thousand feed for a week in a field where we allowed buckwheat to seed out. There were also a few Black Ducks there. The field was right behind our buildings, so if we were careful we could watch them from the gap leading to the field. There was always a bird on guard, though, so we couldn't go very far before they started edging back toward the river.

There are many sub-species of Canada Geese, but we don't concern ourselves with that; we're simply happy to be able to distinguish them from the Brant, a smaller cousin. Besides size, there are a number of distinguishing characteristics. I think the easiest is the voice. A Brant's call is quite different from a Canada's honk; think of it as a Canada with laryngitis. Where Canadas fly in "V" formation (usually), Brant fly in bunches, or in wavering lines, like long skeins of yarn in the wind. While the Canada has a black neck-stocking with white breast, the Brant is black to the waterline. In fact it is sometimes called a Black Brant.

The Brants don't return as early as the Canadas, and are later heading north. Some years, when we are planting our berries in May, there will still be Brant in the river below our fields. It is interesting to watch them; as we move slowly down the field, they will drift away from our shore, out to the channel. Then when we move back up the field, they slowly return. We speculate as to whether they are allowing wind and current to move them, or whether their feet are paddling. Probably some of both, but they seem calm, with no sense of hurry.

Brant rarely come into the fields, their chief food being eel grass. Beginning in 1931, disease devastated the eel grass beds along the Atlantic coast, and the numbers of Brant declined drastically. Some birds managed to survive on sea lettuce and sedge roots. The eel grass has recovered, but the birds' numbers have not returned to the former abundance when they were hunted as a gourmet treat. To pluck the lower stems and roots of the eel grass, they tip bottoms-up, roll the plant into a ball before swallowing, then bob up to catch any pieces floating loose.

We don't often see Canadas and Brant together, but, one day, while crossing the bridge on our road, we saw a mixed flock of Brant, Canadas, Black Ducks, and Herring Gulls close to the bridge. They stayed there as long as the car was moving, even though very slowly; we were able to see clearly the contrasts between the two types of geese.

Goose hunting is allowed now only in the fall. In the early years of the 20th century, there was an open season in the spring as well. Some years ago, one of Everett's uncles told me about goose-hunting in the spring when he was a lad. He was born in 1904, and, in his youth, spring geese were much in demand in the household. He remembered bringing home from the shore a whole cartload of geese, including a few Snow Geese. (We have seen Snow Geese only on a couple of occasions. Probably they were strays from the large flocks that travel farther west of us to gather and feed on the mud flats of the St. Lawrence River before heading to their far northern nesting grounds.)

The feathers and down from that load of birds would be used for mattresses and pillows. The birds aren't usually very fat in the spring, so they wouldn't supply much goose grease. Once the birds were plucked and cleaned, they were packed in the ice house until used as food. After a winter of salt meat, something fresh would be a real treat.

How was it possible to get that many birds in one session of hunting? It was by using a "goose boat." Everett remembers playing in one as a youngster. It was a small one-man scow, decked over to hide the person inside. The hunter could look out through a couple of peepholes and move the boat with hand cranks attached to a paddle wheel on either side. The whole affair was painted white. When rafts of geese were floating near ice cakes, the hunter, moving quietly, could manoeuvre right in among the unsuspecting birds. There was no legal limit on how many could be killed. But those were the days when the birds were needed for food, as they still are in some northern areas. As for sport hunting, we don't care for it.

One thing I always look forward to is seeing them "whiffle." That's a manoeuvre geese sometimes make when they're about to land. Most often they simply glide in, sit down lightly on the water, and give a few shakes to settle their feathers. But occasionally they seem to be full of high spirits—perhaps they're the juveniles—and side-slip and tumble over and over before splashing down. It's quite a sight and sound, when a large number in the flock take part in the fun, all honking and splattering away. It's the flopping around that's called "whiffling."

Another event that gives us great pleasure occurs on a quiet evening when the flock has gathered on the water, near the mouth of the river. They have fed inland, and are now resting for the night where no predators can harm them. They are content. There will be a few gobbling contact sounds throughout the night, but, for now, "God's in his Heaven, all's right with the world."

Small But Mighty

Our family has always liked cats, both as house pets and working animals. Even though we no longer have cattle barns where rats and mice would lurk, we still need cats in our kind of farming. At the moment, we have five—three spayed females that are very good hunters and two neutered males that I call our gentlemen pensioners. I may be maligning those two, but I have never seen either of them with a mouse he caught. They seem to spend most of their time sitting around, looking handsome.

We mow the grass in our orchards several times a year, and the trees have all been mulched at one time or other with straw, timothy hay, and even flax. Neighbours grew the timothy and the flax. The timothy had been left too long in the windrows and there was no market for the flax. Our neighbours needed both removed from their fields, and Everett was happy to oblige. The only drawback to the mulch is that it provides a wonderful place for mice to nest. We need cats there for mouse control, and we also welcome help from hawks, owls, foxes, and skunks. For winter protection, we spread straw on our strawberry fields, and, if we can get enough, around the currant and gooseberry bushes, where it helps control weeds and holds moisture around the plant roots. Then there are the headlands and the hedges—the whole farm is a mouse haven.

It is not a house mouse I'm talking about, but a field mouse, properly called a vole. That name comes from Old Norse, *vollr-mus* (meadow mouse). Fawn to greyish-brown in colour, the field mouse reminds me of a hairy, overstuffed sausage. It is about five-and-a-half to seven-and-a-half inches from head to very short tail, has small, rounded ears and is not as sharp-faced as a house mouse.

Why are they such a problem? Because they do not hibernate but remain active all winter long, running through tunnels they have made in grass or mulches or under the snow, where they are safe from predators. Sometimes we can see signs of their winter activities: they have climbed up a weed stem to eat the seeds, or a fox has dug down beside a stem in hopes of finding something for lunch.

Voles breed all year round; one female in captivity produced seventeen litters in one year. That is not usual, but with five to nine young in a litter, weaned at two weeks and on their own in three, it is easy to understand how their numbers can increase quickly. Females can have several litters before they are three months old. The rate of reproduction with the attendant need for food is what causes such problems for farmers and gardeners.

Prince Edward Island has had its troubles with mice. The town of Souris (which is French for mouse) owes its name to a plague of these little creatures. During the early years of French settlement, the mice invaded regularly, swarming out of the forests and over the farmed lands, eating every growing thing. "Every field of grain from Three Rivers (the Montague, Cardigan, Brudenell area) to Malpeque was made desolate by their ravages," historian A. B. Warburton reported, "and the settlers, all of a sudden, found themselves face to face with starvation." In his *History of Prince Edward Island*, Warburton describes how, after cleaning off the fields, the mice ate everything along the shores and marshes. Many of the creatures drowned, and great rafts of bodies were seen floating out to sea.

Thank Heaven we don't have such numbers here. As it is, we find damage on fruit trees, pine trees, and various ornamentals such as azaleas, rhododendrons, and euonymus. The worst carnage occurred one winter when the snow was so deep, the gooseberry bushes were completely covered. As the snow melted, we expected to find the gooseberries bent down and possibly some branches broken under the snow. Of about two hundred bushes, not one was left! They

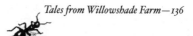

had been chewed to the ground, with just piles of slivers left around the stumps. After a few years, the plants regrew from the base, but that was a really severe pruning.

While the vole causes endless trouble, another meadow mouse, from a different family, never does. It is often called the "kangaroo mouse" because of the way it hops, with its long hind feet and long tail streaming behind it. These mice hibernate, and it is because of that habit that Everett and I saw several of them, not just close at hand, but in hand. Just before freeze-up in two different years, when Everett was moving material for the compost pile into the greenhouse, he found one of these little mice, sound asleep. Each time, he brought the mouse into the house so I could have a good look at it. With its brown and russet colouring, it is much prettier than the vole, and because it doesn't have the same voracious eating habits as the vole does, we enjoyed being able to watch it as it slept. Everett took each of the sleeping creatures back outside and buried it back in the pile, where it would be undisturbed for the rest of its winter sleep.

Enemies of both the kangaroo mouse and the vole include an even smaller creature—the short-tailed shrew. Shrews eat some vegetable matter, but their diet is mostly insects and small mammals, including mice and other shrews. They have specially shaped teeth that form a tweezer- like organ with shearing tips, good for grasping and tearing. Their molars cut through insect shells to get to the juicy inner parts. Above ground, they live in leaf litter and long grass cover. A shrew doesn't have feet as good as the mole for digging, so makes use of other creatures' underground tunnels, as well as above-ground runways. Most shrews have poison glands in their lower jaws, which emit amounts so minute they pose no harm to humans. However, the shrew has enough venom to polish off two hundred mice.

Shrews can eat their own weight in three hours. They must eat constantly, and, if deprived of food for even a day, they will die. They are quite small, about three inches from pointed snout to the end of the tail, with short legs, small ears, and eyes almost hidden in velvety fur. The word "hyperactive" suits these animals; they have a very high metabolic rate, and a heartbeat of up to 1,200 per minute. They are so high-strung they may die of shock if picked up.

When William Shakespeare wrote *The Taming of the Shrew*, he was using a word for his heroine, Kate, that came from Icelandic-Norwegian roots and meant "old man" or "dwarf." As applied to the smallest of our mammals, the name comes from Latin, and is associated with "venomous" because of the poison glands.

But even our cats regard shrews as being in a class by themselves. Sometimes the cats bring shrews home, but never seem interested in eating them. Maybe the poison affects the taste, or perhaps shrews just drop dead when the cat pounces, and as dead meat are no longer fun to play with. In any case, our cats simply leave the shrews on our doorstep, as evidence of their industry.

Making Do

Birds have to work hard these days to find something suitable for nest construction. At one time, they could find hair from the manes and tails of horses and cattle, snippets of wool caught on fences or bushes where sheep passed by, or feathers from barnyard fowl to be used as nest liners. One day, I watched a sparrow trying hard to pull string from a mop I had hung outside to dry. Other birds have gathered stems of alyssum, old leaves from daylilies or iris, twigs from weeping willows, long grass, or straw. We try to help out when we can. At times we have made puddles in our yard so the barn swallows would have enough mud close at hand to make their nests.

Every year, groups of children visit our farm. I save abandoned birds' nests to show the kinds of materials birds use nowadays to replace things no longer available. The inventiveness of those birds reminds me of an expression that came from the Scots tradition of my mother's family: "Everything's grist that comes to the mill." Grist is the grain taken to the mill to be ground, as well as the product after the grinding. The expression meant to make use of whatever is available.

Some of the nests I've found are good examples of that. Example One is what I call a standard nest, very heavy, and made of mud and stems. There must have been lots of rain to keep the soil moist when this one was built. I feel sorry for the birds who built Example Two. It was made of brush and the knobby ends of spruce twigs. Weaving these pieces into a nest, and smoothing it down a bit with mud and grasses, must have been rough work. Some bird must have had a wonderful time constructing Example Three. It was made completely from baler twine, which in a way resembled hair from a cow's tail. Example Four is a real sign of the times; the builders were obviously good recyclers. The nest was made of pieces of plastic, the type found in shopping bags. Example Five is another type that would not have been possible a few years ago. It is one of two we found in which the birds had used discarded, four-inch fibre plant pots, packing mud around them to cover the broken parts. Example Six came from a birdhouse Everett had given our daughter's family in Souris. Tree Swallows had nested in it, and lined it with Seagull feathers, so well-packed they stayed together when the new occupants cleaned it to make it ready for their family.

I have a personal connection to Example Seven, which was not made from the usual materials. It is a smaller nest, probably that of a warbler of some kind. A few years ago, I had chemotherapy following cancer surgery. As a result of the treatment, I lost all my hair, not gradually, but in a short period of time. It was quite a blow to the spirit. What to do with it? Burn it? Put it in the garbage? It was spring, nesting time. I decided to put the hair to use. One day when grandson Jeremy was staying with us, I gave him half of the hair to spread around the gooseberry bushes near the shore. I draped the other half in various places around the hedges and willows near the house. Eventually the hair all disappeared. In the late fall, we found two fragile nests made from my hair, mixed with fluffy seed heads and pod cases from fireweed. I was happy to know the hair had been put to good use.

The varied habitat on our farm provides places for many species of birds to make a home. Song Sparrows and Robins favour the thick spruce hedges. Although robins are highly territorial, one year around the house yard there were four nests that we knew of, with probably more unseen. One of the four was fairly exposed at the end of the hedge between house and barnyard. We try to stay away from nests we know of, but the location of that one made it impossible to do so. Song Sparrows nest on the ground, as well as in the hedge, and often in the strawberry field. Once again it becomes difficult to ignore a nest without leaving it vulnerable to unwanted attention from two- or four-legged creatures.

Twice we have seen nests of Hungarian Partridge. One of these, with twenty eggs, was under a gooseberry bush, abandoned, I'm sorry to say. Perhaps the female became lunch for a fox. The second one was in long grass under an apple tree, with the female on the nest. Once we knew she was there, we left and stayed away. She had a successful hatch. We know they continue to nest here because a couple of times Everett has had to slow the tractor down as he travelled the lane, in order to let a batch of skittering chicks get off the track into the grass. We also know there are foxes around, and we wonder what the odds of survival are for those little birds.

We see so many Blue Jays and Mourning Doves, we think they must also nest on our farm. The jays come to the feeders year-round, though a little less often in summer. One of the strangest sights I have ever seen was a Blue Jay in summer moult. With its head and neck completely bare of feathers, it reminded me of a miniature vulture.

Of course, it's not only birds who need to find homes in the trees on our farm. We used to have a flagpole close to our house. After a few years of being batted around and getting caught in nearby branches, the ends of the flag were quite tattered. One day, our younger grandson and I watched a squirrel fighting with an end of the flag. With a great deal of effort, the squirrel managed to tear off pieces of the flag to take back to its nest. I can remember the fun our grandson derived from the antics of the squirrel, and the joy I had from listening to his laughter. That squirrel had the same idea as the birds do for nest-building: make use of what is available—or, as my mother would say, "Everything's grist that comes to the mill."

WILLOWSHADE FARM
TRYON, P.E.I.

E. K. HOWATT JR.

BERRIES, FRUIT, HONEY

In the Garden

Perennial Favourites

When Everett and I began our first perennial border so many years ago, there were no local nurseries with perennial stock. Even if there had been, we had no money for buying ornamentals then, so we did what gardeners do: we got pieces of plants from kind friends and relatives. Our favourites, which still give us great pleasure, are peonies, delphiniums, and phlox.

Our first peony roots came from my mother and an aunt of Everett's. Those original plants are still producing red, white, and pink blooms in our garden, and have now reached the exalted status of "heritage plants." I dearly love the fragrance of some of these old varieties, *Festiva Maxima*, developed in 1851, being one. I don't really care for them in flower arrangements; I find them difficult to handle, and they last such a short time indoors. I get some of the fragrance I love into the house by floating one bloom in a bowl of water. "Enough is as good as a feast."

The name peony comes from the mists of Greek mythology. Paeon, a pupil of Aesclepius, the god of healing, aroused his teacher's jealousy by healing wounds of Pluto and Mars. Aesclepius plotted Paeon's death, but Pluto saved Paeon from the fate of mortals by changing him into the plant he had used to save Pluto's life. The plant became known botanically as *Paeonia officinalis*. That second part indicates it was used as a medicine. We find peonies in pink, white, red, and, in the woody forms, yellow, but it was a red peony that had the original designation.

There are now hundreds of registered varieties that have been developed from the original species found growing wild in temperate regions of Eurasia. China was a prime source of both woody (tree) peonies and the more usual herbaceous types. So important are they in the culture and history of China that the Chinese call the tree peony "the King of Flowers," the symbol of royalty, wealth, and rank. The herbaceous form is called "the Prime Minister of All Flowers."

We have had one tree peony for many years, but it is not very hardy. Some years the buds will overwinter, and we have some beautiful fragrant flowers like yellow organdy. Other years the plant dies to the ground and has to start all over again; its stems must be two years old in order to bloom. This is in contrast to the herbaceous peonies, which always die back in winter and bloom on the current year's growth.

We prize peonies for their flowers, and must work at keeping them healthy. So I am somewhat amazed when I find that in some places enough peonies were grown to be used as food, as well as medicine. The roots were used in soups in Siberia; in England in the Middle Ages they accompanied roast pork on the tables of the rich. The common people were lucky to get some of the seeds to use as seasoning. The Ale Wife in *Pier's Plowman* (1362) says, "I have pepper and peony seed and a pound of garlic and a farthingsworth of fennel seed for the fasting days."

While the peony is strictly a perennial, delphiniums and phlox both have annual forms. Both types of phlox share the same name, but the annual form of delphiniums is called larkspur. The name delphinium comes from a Greek word meaning "a little dolphin" or "a dolphin snout." That isn't as easy to see as the lark's claw (spur) in the annuals. There were some thirty species of larkspur native to Europe, some of which naturalized very readily in North America. Larkspurs have poisonous qualities; where they have naturalized in the United States, they are second to loco weed in causing the deaths of grazing cattle. The name *Espuela del caballero* (cavalier's spur) given to the plant by Spanish-Californians tells us how far it travelled. But long before that time, its poisonous qualities were put to use in Europe. The Romans called it *Herba pedicularia* because of its use in treating head lice, body lice, and itch mites. Some 1,800 years later, the Duke of Wellington issued a larkspur delousing solution to his troops, giving rise to the claim that the plant helped win the Battle of Waterloo in 1815.

Who says plant history is dull?

The first of our delphiniums came to our garden, as did the peonies, from relatives. With lots of lime they did well, some of them growing more than six feet tall. In recent years Everett has been starting some from seed. This has given us some lovely colours and forms, even one almost black, but so far they don't seem to have the stamina of the old-fashioned ones. Of one thing we can be fairly sure: if the delphiniums are particularly good, there'll be a thundering rain storm to break the stems over whatever support we've given them.

Phlox doesn't have quite as romantic a name as peony, delphinium, or larkspur. The Roman naturalist Pliny used the name "phlox" about 2,000 years ago for another plant, but the Swedish botanist Linnaeus borrowed the name, which comes from a Greek word for flame, for the phlox we know today. Linnaeus thought the furled buds looked like little torches, which proves that imagination goes a long way in naming plants.

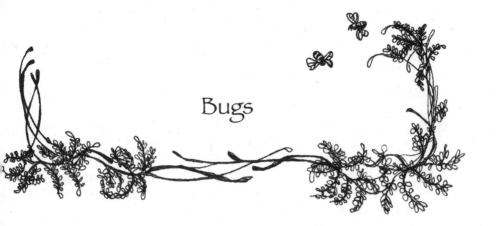

Bugs

Ants, aphids, and ladybird beetles—that could almost be the first line of a song. You might almost add that, like love and marriage, you can't have one without the other. Despite their differences, these creatures are all interconnected. And, despite their tiny size, they all have a profound impact on many of us humans, for good and for ill.

Ants may be one of the earliest insects a child will learn to recognize out-of-doors, along with flies and butterflies. Just sit a child on the ground, a piece of food in hand, and a hungry ant will come along. When one does, we can be fairly sure there will be many more, the reason being that as an ant travels, it lays down a scent trail that others can follow. Each ant does the same in turn, reinforcing the scent, so no time is lost in going to the source of food.

A conservative estimate says there are several thousands of ant species worldwide; another says 6,000, with about 180 in Canada. They range from tiny to very large, and from inoffensive to mean and nasty—that, of course, is to our way of thinking. I shall give you an example of ones we consider nasty, at the same time recognzing that this is the way they have to live.

One year, we decided to increase the number of our beehives to fill the demand for honey. We realized we'd be short of pasturage, even if we scattered the hives around our farm. We wanted a place sheltered from wind and sprays; with wild blossoms and fresh water available, and away from humans or animals that bees might bother. We found a place on a friend's land, the edge of a cut-over woodlot, with lots of wild shrubs and flowers. It was a lovely place for bees, or so we thought. With our friend's permission, we set up three hives with new packages—boxes of thousands of bees, including queens.

Within a few days, all queens were laying. Things looked good.

Then disaster struck in the form of big black ants. They were strong and fierce enough to overpower the adult bees and actually pull the larvae from the cells. Those ants liked fresh meat. Even the queens were gone, the hives completely ruined. We tracked the culprits to a nest under a rotting log. We always check for signs of above-ground nests before setting up hives, but hadn't thought of turning over that log. We haven't taken hives off the farm since then. Instead, we plant more forage for the bees and keep them home.

In contrast to those meat eaters, some ants are strictly vegetarian, gardeners who grow their food underground. We would call them mushroom eaters. They cut pieces of leaves from plants, and take them into special areas of the nest to compost the leaves. On that compost grows a fungus that is food for the ants.

Other ants are farmers who look after other insects and eat what they produce. Just as dairy farmers take care of cows, some species of ants have "aphid cows," which require what I think is a fairly complicated form of management. They may be small insects, but they are very smart and their actions make me think of verses from Proverbs: "Go to the ant, thou sluggard; consider her ways and be wise: Which having no guide, overseer or ruler, provideth her meat in the summer, and gathereth her food in the harvest."

In autumn, the farmer ants collect aphid eggs, which they store over the winter in their nest. In spring, they take the eggs outdoors to hatch. They produce two or three generations (with aphids that doesn't take long), and then take the adult aphids into the nest to feed on plant roots for ten to twenty generations. The aphids suck nutrients from the plant roots, then exude honey dew, which is almost a sugar syrup. This the ants drink, and the cycle continues.

One underground ants' nest in front of our house has been there for more than fifty years. At first, its exit was just under the edge of the wooden verandah. We subsequently replaced the wood with clay tiles on the ground, but every year we can be sure to see ants come swarming out and floating away, like smoke on the air, when the time for mating has come. It is quite a sight to see such great numbers of the insects, knowing that most of them won't see another day. Birds will eat many on the wing. The young males, having served their purpose, will die. Many of the newly mated females (queens) will fall prey to toads, snakes, shrews, or birds on the ground.

If they survive all those hazards, the mated female (queens) will chew or rub off their wings, which are no longer needed, and find a place to lay their first eggs. The queens will look after the offspring until they are adults able to take on the work of an ant colony. Then the queens will do nothing but eat and produce eggs for the rest of their lives. Most of the eggs produce neuters, or workers. At a certain time, winged males and females will be produced to go out and start new nests all over again.

As with ants, there are thousands of species of aphids, in all colours imaginable: black, red, pink, green, yellow, lavender, brown, grey, white. The book I call my "Bug Bible" has specific information on more than two hundred species in North America. A few live on one kind of plant only, but many like a varied diet. Some spend winter on one type of plant, and summer on another. Their numbers can build up very quickly, because they can reproduce without the services of a male. Males don't appear until late in the season to help produce eggs that will overwinter. In frost-free areas, aphids can continue year-round without males, producing a new generation every seven to ten days.

That's bad news for many people who live on this Island. The green peach aphid loves potato leaves. That in itself mightn't be too bad, but these aphids are like malaria mosquitoes, leaving something unwanted behind when they eat. In the case of the potato, the aphids transmit a virus that is very harmful to the plant. On come the pesticides to try to control the aphids. Some generations of aphids have wings, and, with the right winds, they can travel far. Considering their reproductive capability, they can become really troublesome.

Sparrows, Chickadees, and even Hummingbirds will eat aphids, but the champion aphid-eater of the lot is the ladybug.

From the time our children were small, they have known the importance of ladybugs. If they found one, they would bring it to me so I could put it on plants in my flower room. There was only one time that we saw a group of ladybugs that had overwintered. They were under boards from an old building that was being removed.

They had already "converged"; they were tightly packed together. We watched as the mass expanded and became a living, moving carpet of bright colours.

The larvae look very different from the adults. They are humpy, bumpy, and carrot-shaped. Some have bristly backs, black and orange, or dark blue and red. Depending on the species, an adult can lay up to 1,500 eggs within two months.

Both larvae and adults are real eating machines. A larva can eat up to twenty-five aphids a day, an adult fifty to a hundred. Their numbers are quite cyclic. As aphids increase, so do the beetles that eat them. Then beetle numbers decline until the aphid population rises again. It's a matter of nature maintaining a balance.

What we call ladybugs should properly be called ladybird beetles. The name goes back to the Middle Ages in Europe, when it was dedicated to the Virgin Mary in recognition of the great service it did in protecting crops by eating harmful insects. The original name was Our Lady's Beetle.

Do you remember this nursery rhyme?

Ladybug, ladybug, fly away home
Your house is on fire and your children are all gone
All except one and her name is Anne
And she crept under the frying pan.

This verse comes from the late 1600s; the original one had a warming pan, not a frying pan. Warming pans were covered utensils on a long handle, used to hold live coals to help dry out and warm up damp beds in unheated bedrooms. The verse is connected to a story about the British Royal Family of that era: at the time of the Great Fire of London in 1666, Charles II was King. He was succeeded a few years later by his brother, James II, who had two daughters, Mary and Anne, by his first wife. His second wife gave birth to a boy, also named James. The baby's half-sister, Anne, was in the palace at the time of his birth. Rumours spread that the baby boy had been smuggled into the queen's bed in a warming pan. The other half-sister, Mary, then living in Holland, wrote to Anne questioning the legitimacy of the birth, for until then Mary was in line for the throne, and eventually became Queen. Anne also became Queen, but only for a few years. She gave birth to nineteen children, only one of whom survived infancy—and that child died at the age of eleven.

How the ladybug enters into the story, and which historical figure it represents, makes for a good guessing game. It's something to think about the next time you see a ladybug—or, for that matter, an aphid or an ant.

Not Wanted in the Garden

Can you imagine a garden where there were no cutworms or ear-wigs or white grubs to thin out or mess up your prized plants? Add to that list of pests a member of the mollusc family. That family provides some of my favourite foods—oysters, mussels, and clams—and one of my least favourite garden inhabitants. The outcast is the slug. Along with cutworms, earwigs, and white grubs, slugs provoke gardeners into uttering many nasty words.

Cutworms are the larvae (grubs) of a number of night-flying moths. They overwinter as partly grown larvae in soil, under plant trash, or in clumps of grass. In the past, when people applied lots of manure to gardens, cutworms were generally much more of a prob-lem than they are now, although I imagine some gardeners would say they are worse. If so, it is because the creatures are finding places where they can shelter for the winter.

The grubs start feeding in the spring once plant growth begins, and only at night. Once fully grown, they burrow into the soil to pu-pate. The adult moths appear in the summer, lay the eggs that hatch into the small larvae that overwinter, and off we go again. Some years, the moth population jumps when a flight of adults arrives on southwest winds from the United States, the same winds that bring unwanted corn ear-worm moths.

Home gardeners can protect transplants from grubs by using col-lars made from slices of paper towel rollers, paper cups, aluminum foil—anything that will keep hungry larvae from getting near the plants at soil level. When it comes to seeded crops such as beans, which seem to be a particular target, a keen eye and a sharp hoe are the best bet. Sometimes we find the grubs in corn and vine crops, but, by hoeing regularly when the plants are young, we have little trouble. One English garden writer once said the best way to get rid of grubs was "to dispatch them with a No. 10 Wellie." Translated, that means: step on them with your rubber boot (Wellington).

The June bugs we find have overwintered as pupae in the ground. They hatch in spring, and remain hidden during the day in leaf debris or plant trash. I sometimes find adults when working the flower beds early in the day. At night, they feed on foliage of ash, birch, butternut, poplar, oak, willow, and other hardwoods and ornamentals. When I look at that list, I realize our yard is June Bug Heaven. The females, once mated, enter the soil to lay each egg in a separate ball of earth several inches below the surface of the sod. They choose sod because it may be three to four years before the full growth cycle is over, and during that time the larva needs a constant supply of roots on which to feed.

The egg will hatch in two to three weeks; the young grub feeds until fall, burrows into the earth for winter, and moves up the next spring to feed on roots of various plants. If the grubs survive a second year of feeding, they burrow down for another winter and go into a pupal stage, hatching the next spring as an adult. During the second year of feeding, the white larvae, with dark head, will be quite plump and at least an inch long. This is when skunks can really do us a favour by digging up and eating the grubs. Because a lawn is in sod continuously, there's bound to be a crop of new larvae every year, eating the roots of the lawn grass. Lawn owners may not like skunks, but they are less hazardous than the poisons needed to kill grubs if there are no smelly critters available.

Another pest, the earwig, appeared on our Island only in the past eight to ten years, and I became aware of it on our farm about four years ago. The name of this insect came from an old idea that it crawled out of wigs and into the ears of wig wearers. This was a strongly held belief in Europe, where the critter has been a garden pest for hundreds of years. In England in the 1700s, various methods were advocated for their control: "In trees hang old boots well stopt with hay." (Imagine your favourite fruit tree ornamented with a batch of running shoes.) Or "hang hoggs hoofs, bowls of tobacco pipes and lobster claws on the tops of sticks among plants and kill the vermin that lodge on them every morning." In my opinion, simple baits from which the "vermin" can be removed are still the best way to deal with these insects.

Of the four pests I mentioned in the beginning, the one I dislike most is the slug. The English poet Coleridge (of "Ancient Mariner" fame) spoke of the "slug leaving its lair" as a sign of spring. It's a sign I can well do without. A few fat toads to eat the slugs would be a much more acceptable sign. The family name of the slug, *gastropoeda*, comes from the Greek, and can be loosely translated as "a stomach on a foot." That description certainly applies. Slugs are real eating machines. The mouth part, called a radule, is like a file that is continuously rasping. Some slugs eat animal matter, but it is the plant-eaters that really annoy me.

Because of this pest, I haven't planted salvias for several years. Slugs will strip them completely. Their other favourites include marigolds and hostas. I am prepared to fight for the marigolds, and the hostas usually manage to grow strong enough to keep ahead of the slugs, but it would be nice to have a few leaves without holes.

The reason for our slug problem is that the walls of old sandstone around our house and some flower beds provide damp hidey-holes for them and their eggs. I must admit, though I hate the sight of the slugs, their eggs are beautiful, like tiny pearls.

Without using poison bait, and with no lovely fat toads to help us, we must try to control the slugs by drying them out. The slug has a rudimentary shell buried in its body tissue, showing its relationship to the molluscs, but has no external shell to protect its slimy body from drying out. To keep from tearing its body, it secretes that slime to give it a smooth path on which to travel. We protect our plants by spreading material that will hinder the slug's movement—wood ashes, crushed eggshells, or diatomaceous earth. The diatomaceous earth is made from fossil shells of tiny marine creatures. The silica in the shells cuts into the skin of the slugs, causing them to lose fluid. I've been wondering whether the fine grit that Grandpa used to get from the shore for his hens might serve the same purpose.

We don't have problems with slugs in our vegetable fields. Even though the foliage of some plants might provide some shelter, it's not a permanent hiding place like the stone walls. As well, the clay mulch in the cultivated fields makes it difficult for slugs to move around. It would take too much of those vital juices to smooth the path.

We have flower beds on top of the stone wall just outside our back door. Some of my favourite perennial "sniffing" plants are there, as well as a few special annuals. That means that I don't have to go far to start my morning ritual of picking up slugs, throwing them onto the tiles and stepping on them. It amused me one day to overhear my grandson Jonathan say to someone in the house, "Gran's outdoors, jumping on slugs again." That seems to be the one treatment that works for all four of those critters that I'd rather not have in our gardens.

A Simple Earwig Trap

Take a shallow, covered dish. Half-fill it with water, and add a tablespoon of vegetable oil, a few drops of dish detergent (to reduce surface tension), and a small piece of fruit or a few drops of fish oil. Make holes in the lid so that insects can crawl in. Remove the "vermin" every morning.

To Gladden the Heart

Some of my favourite plants grow in beds on top of and around the walls near our back door. Among them are lavender and thyme. A third one, rosemary, cannot winter out-of-doors, so I plant it in pots that stay outside in summer and move into the plant room for the cold months. For generations all three herbs have been used to "gladden the heart," and that is one reason I grow them. A sprig, pinched off and tucked in a pocket as I go out to work, can give a lift to my spirits any time I come upon it.

Lavender's blue, dilly dilly, lavender's green
When I am king, dilly dilly, you shall be queen.

It's been a long time since I have heard this children's song about one of the most popular and best-loved herbs. The name probably came from a Latin word, *lavare*, meaning to wash. The Romans, who knew a good thing found growing under their noses, scented their bath water with lavender. Long before they did so, the Egyptians and Phoenicians used lavender as perfume.

Lavender is called a sub-shrub, but never attains that status in our garden; I am happy if it survives and grows well enough to provide some flowering stems. Some species have white flowers, some pink, but the usual colour is lavender-blue. What else should it be? In England in the Middle Ages, both men and women wore the flower stem quilted into their hats to "comfort the brains." It had a reputation as a tranquilizer, though I doubt it was as powerful as claimed by one herbalist, who said that lions and tigers in zoos grew docile from the scent of lavender water. That hard-working monarch, Queen Elizabeth I, used a different form to settle her down. She was very fond of lavender conserve, a preparation of the flowers in sugar.

Rosemary, *ros maris*, the dew of the sea—these names were given to this plant because of its habit of growing close to the Mediterranean Sea, and because of the dew-like appearance of the blossoms when seen from a distance. Rosemary has the designation *officinalis*, meaning an official medicine, because from earliest times its medicinal virtues were recognized. In Ancient Greece, students wore sprigs of rosemary in their hair because it was supposed to strengthen the memory; thus it became a symbol of remembrance. In Shakespeare's *Hamlet*, rosemary is part of Ophelia's bouquet in the mad scene where she says, "There's Rosemary, that's for remembrance; pray you, love, remember."

In Medieval times, people burned resinous rosemary in sick chambers to purify the air, and spread branches of it in the law courts as protection against jail fever. At the same time, judges carried rosemary and thyme in "nosegays" so they wouldn't have to breathe the foul air. During the Black Plague of 1665, rosemary was carried in the handles of walking sticks or in pouches, to be sniffed when travelling through suspicious areas. This herb certainly has powerful attributes.

In my kitchen, rosemary goes in meat dishes and stews, and I can always snip the fresh herb off potted plants. I had one for more than twenty years. It became quite straggly at the end of its days. I have two large ones now and am trying to control them by judicious pruning, but I know they will never be as neat and regulated as the ones we see in florist shops at Christmastime, advertised as Rosemary Topiary Trees. I'd like to see what one of those looks like a year later.

Our rosemary plants have blue flowers, but some species have white ones; a friend has one of those. A Spanish legend explains the variation: during the flight of the Holy Family into Egypt, Mary spread her cloak over a white-flowered shrub under which they were sheltering. (In their native habitat, rosemary plants grow up to six feet high.) In the morning, the flowers had taken on the blue colour of Mary's cloak. It is no wonder that this herb became one of the plants grown in gardens dedicated to the Virgin Mary.

Thyme is another perennial herb native across the Mediterranean region and into Asia. It was spread widely and is now naturalized in many parts of North America, including Prince Edward Island. According to local folklore, it was introduced here intentionally in the 19th century, in early grass mixtures. Thyme was considered an improver of poor thin soils. It would give cover and gradually add humus that would allow other plants to move in. Thyme grows best on thin sandy soil and cannot grow among plants that hold moisture around their foliage. When these move in, the thyme gradually disappears.

At one time, we tried a jar of honey that was produced from thyme growing on Mt. Hymettus in Greece. It has been famous for hundreds of years, and is still exported around the world. We found it too strong, almost medicinal. We were prejudiced, we admit, since we think the honey produced on our farm is among the best. (No conceit there, of course!)

The name, thyme, was derived from a Greek word for courage, so, during the Crusades, ladies embroidered sprigs of thyme on scarves for their knights, to help keep their spirits up. Linnaeus, the father of binomial nomenclature of plants, claimed that thyme tea would dispel the fumes of drunkenness. That seems to validate a claim made many years earlier that thyme "removed headache occasioned by inebriation." There is a much more pleasant mental picture of thyme in a poem by Rudyard Kipling, describing the sunny hillsides of the Mediterranean, redolent with the scent of thyme "like the perfume of the dawn of Paradise." I'll try to keep that in mind when I'm working around the thyme plants on the wall at our back door.

Plants that Come from Away

When people on this Island describe someone not native to the province, they use the term "come from away." Granny had her own designation: such people were "from over across." We have many plants on the Island that are "come-from-aways"—some much loved and some much maligned.

The dandelion fits both categories: loved if you happen to be a beekeeper, maligned if you strive for an all-green lawn or golf course. We happen to love those little yellow flowers that have been described as soldiers with golden helmets, parading across lawns and fields. For beekeepers in the springtime, a mass of dandelions in full bloom is a gladsome sight. The blooms are one of the earliest wild flowers available to the bees, and are a good source of the pollen that a newly hatched brood needs to develop into a strong hive.

When we see those masses of bright yellow blooms, on lawns and roadsides and in fields, it is hard to believe they weren't here until introduced by European settlers. Dandelions (from the French *dent-de-lion* or lion's tooth) were native to Europe and Asia. The first part of its botanical name, *Taraxacum officinale*, comes from Arabic; the second part indicates use as a medicine that could be sold in pharmacies.

There are few references to the plant from Greek and Roman times, though it is said that Hecate, the Greek goddess of the underworld, fed a salad of dandelions to Theseus before he went out to kill the beast Minotaur. By the 16th century, the dandelion was well-established in European apothecaries, where it was known as *herba taraxacon* or *herba urinaria* because of its diuretic effects. Those effects gave it the folk name in French of *pissenlit*; in English, piss-a-bed.

The Encyclopedia of Herbs, published in 1981, says the dandelion is one of the most useful European herbs. "It is an extremely effective medicinal plant, being possibly the safest, most active plant diuretic and one of the best herbs known to treat liver complaint."

Both roots and leaves of the dandelion are edible. The leaves are much more palatable if you blanch them by covering them with straw or old buckets. We're usually so busy in the spring, that, by the time we get around to picking them, the leaves are too bitter. The roots can be boiled as a vegetable, or dried and ground to make a coffee substitute. Some years ago, my son thought we should give the coffee idea a try. After digging, washing, drying, grinding, and brewing, I am quite prepared to drink water instead. I don't need coffee that badly.

Though I am glad to welcome the bright yellow flowers to feed the bees, I'd be happier if dandelions would stay out of the lawns. In my early years on this farm, I used to walk around and cut out the crowns. To help me out, my father-in-law made a long-handled tool for me, like an asparagus-cutting knife. But still there were dandelions, robust ones, with two, four, eight crowns where once there was one. What was going on? Investigation was in order.

I discovered that dandelions have cells called *parenchyma*, which literally means "poured around." Any small part of the plant left in the ground can make specialized cells, usually two stems for every one cut off. This form of plant cloning gave me the multiple crowns in the lawns.

Now that I've learned my lesson, I take a sturdy fork and lever out the dandelions while the lawn is still fairly soft in the spring. When I am through, it sometimes looks as though a demented mole has been at work. What I can't get out, the lawn mower can control—maybe. Perhaps the best way to get rid of the plant is to eat it.

Red and white clovers, which also come "from away," are generally better accepted than dandelions, although golf course greenskeepers are again an exception. I don't share their concern, but then, I'm not a golfer.

In fact, we are always happy when we see our neighbour has cattle to pasture. The animals keep the field grazed so the clover will bloom, and make up for the lack of it in our own kind of farming. Clover is important on our farm because it allows us to produce clover honey. White clover provides a mild, light-coloured liquid honey, which turns white when granulated.

Honey bees may also visit red clover, but they have problems with it: the tube leading to the nectar is too long, and the bee's tongue can't reach the nectar. Even bumblebees have trouble with red clover flowers, although they have learned to make a back door. They reach the nectar by cutting a hole at the base of the floret. Honey bees are known to take advantage of the help.

Years ago, I visited a home where the hosts offered me a taste of "home-made honey," a syrup made by boiling red and white clover blossoms with sugar water, and then straining the mixture. It did look like honey, and for those unused to the real thing, it was probably quite satisfactory. I was brought up on the genuine article. Every fall, Dad would buy a forty-pound bucket of honey from the supply produced by bees at the Charlottetown Experimental Farm. Later, I had the good fortune to marry a beekeeper. As a matter of fact, the first gift he ever gave me was a container of honey from his bees.

Cattle are not the only beneficiaries of clover. Both red and white kinds have provided food and medicine for humans for hundreds of years. In fact, clovers are one of the most important survival foods. They are common, easily recognized, and widespread. Both dried flowers and seeds, made into porridge or a form of bread, were famine food in Ireland and Scotland.

Druid priests and medicine men in early England considered the plants sacred and powerful. They carried them to ward off evil spirits when travelling through suspect places. It sounds to me like an early version of carrying a four-leaf clover for luck. For Christians, the leaves symbolized the Trinity, the three-in-one, as in the shamrock.

The plants' generic name, *Trifolium*, reflects the three-part leaves. It was a family that soon became established in many parts of North America following European settlement. Native peoples called the white clover "white man's foot." The honey bees, *Apis mellifera*, which seemed to accompany the clover, were also immigrants.

Natives called them "white man's fly."

Queen Anne's lace is a third come-from-away that, like the clover and the dandelion, has established itself firmly in Prince Edward Island soil.

The scientific name for this plant, *Daucus carota*, comes from Greek and Latin names for a wild carrot found in hedgerows in Europe, a plant long used as both food and medicine. In the 16th century, German horticulturists developed the root crop we call carrot, and its use quickly spread. In July 1631, a seed order sent from England to the Massachusetts colony included one pound of "carrett" seed.

The early wild form was used as a medicine in the treatment of kidney stones, and the seeds were eaten to treat flatulence. Three physician-naturalists of the 1st and 2nd century AD had varied uses for the plant. Dioscorides felt those who used it "would not be hurt by all manner of venomous beasts." Galen said it was "a certain force to procure lust." Pliny's idea was somewhat similar: "It winneth love." Culpeper and Gerard, two herbalists of the 1600s, highly recommended the roots "for the breaking of wind though experience teaches they breed it first."

Present-day botanists don't all agree on the relationship between the vegetable carrot and the wild form. One source says that seedlings from the first carrots grown in America escaped to the wild and reverted to the plant we call Queen Anne's lace. Another maintains that there is little possibility of that, though the wild may cross with the cultivated form, causing problems in commercial crops.

Queen Anne's lace belongs to the family *Umbelliferae* (think of little umbrellas), alternatively called *Apiaceae*. The plant takes its common name from an English monarch, Anne, who lived from 1665 to 1714. She is said to have pricked her finger while making lace. If you look into the heart of the main cluster of these flowers, you will see a tiny deep-red or purple flower, representing the drop of blood from Queen Anne's finger. According to folklore, eating those little red flowers in the centre would prevent epileptic seizures. I'm not sure about that, but the red flower is a good way to separate Queen Anne's lace from one of its less desirous relatives, the poison hemlock.

Some people think that Queen Anne's lace is a pernicious weed. I happen to love it. It is one of my favourite flowers. Picture a lovely sunny day in late July or early August. Along the roadside, a drift of snowy-white Queen Anne's lace mingles with a few bright blue blooms of chicory and spots of yellow hawkweed.

In fact, some of our plant immigrants brighten the Island landscape from spring to late summer—dandelions in spring, clovers from spring into summer, and Queen Anne's lace from mid- to late summer. They provide food for the soul and, in some cases, for the body, too.

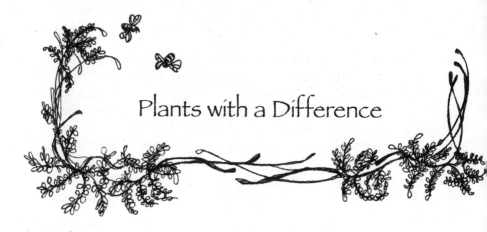

Plants with a Difference

Even before Everett finished building the glass house on the southeast corner of our porch, he wanted a larger one, with more space for plants. I'm sure if we had more room, it would still be overflowing with plants. Any true gardener knows the feeling: there's always another plant it would be nice to have. We use the greenhouse mostly to overwinter plants that we will move outdoors for the summer—bay trees, rosemary, and the very large jade trees. Our Ponderosa lemon, which we have had for forty-nine years, a couple of much younger Calmondin oranges, and a fig tree keep company with clivia, bougainvillaea and cactus of various kinds, before we can find room for geraniums and other house plants, as well as a few others that are out of the ordinary. Among these are a starfish cactus and an epiphyllum cactus. They came to us in quite an unorthodox way. The manner of their coming I will tell you later.

First, I want to explain why we find those plants so fascinating. The word "starfish" aptly describes the shape of the flowers on a plant whose proper name is *Stapelia*. Linnaeus gave it that name as a tribute to Johannes Bodaeus von Stapel of Amsterdam. There are a number of varieties, with flowers ranging from two to three inches across to a very large one of fourteen to sixteen inches from point to point. Ours has blooms of three to four inches. It belongs to the milkweed family, and is related to the hoya and the rosary vine. The stems are knobby and bumpy. They reach upwards so far, then flop over. Given a chance, they will root at the tip, and repeat the growing up and flopping procedure. In this way, they can move from place to place outdoors, as in their native habitat of South Africa. They're a real travelling plant.

Another common name for the members of this genus is "carrion flowers," because the blooms smell like rotting meat or fish. The smell attracts the carrion or blowflies that pollinate the plants. We saw how this feature works when I took a plant in bloom out to our on-farm market so that others could see the interesting flowers. (Fortunately, we can enjoy the blooms without sniffing them.) Some blow-flies found them, and, within a few days, the centre of the bloom was crawling with tiny blow-fly maggots. Not to worry. There was nothing there on which the maggots could feed, and while they were there, they did their duty, pollinating the blossom, which closed up and dropped off.

The plant ovary is not at the base of the blossom, but inside the stem of the plant, possibly as a protection measure in a harsh environment. After a full year, a seed pod appeared in a location that seemed to have little bearing to that of the blossom. Torpedo-shaped, and about six inches long (it reminded me of okra), the ripened pod split lengthways to reveal closely packed seeds on parachutes, just like those of the milkweed plants. It is relatively easy to start new stapelia from cuttings, so we didn't try germinating the seed, although an interested relative did, without success.

The blooms of the epiphyllum cactus have no stems at all. The name, from the Greek, can be translated as "upon the leaves," referring to the way in which the flowers come directly from nodes on the flattened, fleshy stems. Many think of cactus as growing in dry, sandy soils, but these plants are tree dwellers in their native home in southern Mexico. They are not parasites on the trees, but epiphytes, anchoring themselves on the wood and living on nutrients from plant and insect debris that lands around them. This is a characteristic they share with many orchids. Another thing they share is the beauty of the flowers, which leads to a common name of the epiphyllum, orchid cactus. What a sight it would be to come upon one of these in bloom, away up in the treetop in a rain forest.

The epiphyllums have been subjects for much hybridizing, giving a range of colours from white and yellow through to brilliant reds, with blooms up to twelve inches across. Our plant has beautiful, clear red flowers, as big as the palm of my hand. It does best in a hanging pot; when the sun shines from above, through the tissue-like petals, the flowers are aflame. Though they are cactus, they don't care for direct sunlight. They prefer filtered light, like that coming through the leaves of trees. In summer, we hang them outdoors in the trees, though there might not be as much humidity as they like. Too much nitrogen will produce a lovely green plant, but not much in the way of bloom. Ours may look somewhat ratty, but we do get blossoms. The plants have a habit of starting more buds than they can properly develop, and the extra ones drop off. This same phenomenon appears in other plants as well. We are used to seeing it in apple trees. We expect what we call a "June drop" even after pollination. In the case of the orchid cactus, the buds don't open. It took a while before we understood that this is a part of its normal growth. It seems to be a case of quality, rather than quantity.

Now, how do we happen to own these two quite different plants? For that, we have to thank a relative of my mother, Cousin Joe, who had lost a leg on the battlefields of France during the Great War, and as a result wore an artificial leg. On his return home, he began farming again, and travelled very little. To my knowledge, the only place he went off-Island was to Camp Hill Veterans' Hospital in Halifax to have his "stump" and "tin leg" attended to. So we were very surprised when, on retiring from farming, he decided to visit his older brother, Dan. This happened a few years after Everett and I were married.

Dan had served in the Great War as well, but moved to the United States after the war, married there, and became an American citizen. As such, he served in the Second World War, along with his two sons, one of whom died of wounds. When Dan retired, he moved to Arizona. (Dan didn't get the title of "Cousin," I guess, because he rarely appeared here, whereas "Cousin Joe" was a regular fixture in our family.) It was on his visit to Arizona that Cousin Joe saw stapelia travelling along the foundation of Dan's home. Where he found the epiphyllum I don't know. Cousin Joe, who never before, by word or deed, had ever paid attention to Everett and me, surprised us greatly by bringing plant cuttings home to us.

Everett and I knew well the paperwork hassles associated with bringing plants from the States into Canada—phyto-sanitary certificates for the plants, import permits from the federal authorities, and so on. We asked Cousin Joe how he had managed so easily. His response: "Ask me no questions, I'll tell you no lies." From that, we got the idea, which we retain to this day, that the cuttings of the starfish and orchid cactus crossed the border inside Cousin Joe's tin leg.

Licorice-Related

I have been fond of licorice from the time a policeman introduced me to the flavour when I was a small child. At the time, our family lived on Spring Park Road in Charlottetown. My Dad was working regular hours then, and he would arrive home for supper at the same time every evening, with little variation. One summer evening, before I was three years old, I was waiting for him to appear. Mother was busy getting supper ready and looking after my baby sister. My older sister and brother probably were supposed to be keeping an eye on me, but I eluded them. I decided to go looking for Dad. I knew the direction from which he would come, so set off walking, all the way to Euston Street. No sign of Dad. Then I walked down Euston to Pownal Street. Still no sign of him, and by this time I was completely lost. Some Good Samaritan, noticing my predicament, took me to the police station on Kent Street. Fortunately for me, the officer in charge was our neighbour across the brook. He recognized me, and said he would take me home when his shift ended, which would be fairly soon. Since there were few private telephones in the town at that time, he had no quick way of informing my parents of my whereabouts. The officers sat me on top of a desk and fed me ice cream and licorice candy until the time came to take me home. I don't remember much else about that incident—just the taste of the licorice.

Incidentally, the policeman neighbour and his wife, Kate, were Irish Catholics, strong Catholics, who went against the trend of the times by being very good friends to my parents, Scots Presbyterian Protestants. That was quite a mixture, but a very friendly one. One time Kate sold my parents tickets for the annual parish supper at the Church of the Most Holy Redeemer. She made sure Mother and Dad were well looked after. When it was time for dessert, she arrived with a beautiful piece of lemon meringue pie for Dad. She told him, proudly, that it was a slice from the pie that had been set aside for the Bishop. That, I guess, was the greatest accolade she could give him.

Once that friendly policeman turned me on to licorice, I continued to enjoy it. In later years, I learned some facts about the plants from which the flavour is derived. As it turns out, there are a number of such plants. What I would call the true form belongs to the genus *Glychrrhiza*, of which three varieties are commonly grown for the root that is used to make candy and liqueurs, to flavour tobacco, to put a head of foam on beer, to sweeten soft drinks, and to provide pharmaceutical products with anti-inflammatory properties. And you thought, as did I, licorice was only good in candy! The reason licorice is so widely used is that it is fifty times sweeter than sugar. I have had some imported licorice that was so sweet I could not eat it.

Another licorice-flavoured plant caught my attention because of its association (so I thought) with Biblical times. This was anise hyssop. Hyssop was a plant that the people of Israel used in many rituals. At the time of the first Passover, they used it to sprinkle blood on the doorposts of the Children of Israel, to distinguish them from the Egyptians. Hyssop has remained as one of the bitter herbs used at the Passover Supper. Hyssop was also the herb mixed in the sour wine offered to Christ on the Cross (John 19:29). There are conflicting stories as to what kind of hyssop it was. One source says it was a form of oregano or marjoram, both well-known herbs native to the Mediterranean area. Another source claims it is related to the equally well-known family of mints.

To further confuse the matter, it turns out that the anise hyssop I have chosen to grow is not a hyssop at all, but an *agastache*, so called because the flower head looks like the head on wheat, which is what the Greek name means. The plant is listed as a perennial, so I could plant it in hopes of seeing it in the same place another year. But that hasn't been the case. It acts like a fairly hardy annual, with seedlings coming up in various places, even between the old sandstones on the wall. Once it decides to grow it becomes a sturdy plant, with rose-purple-blue flower heads much loved by the bees.

I certainly don't mind the taste or smell of licorice, and the leaves of the agastache give me great pleasure. To pick one, crush it between my fingers, then sniff, is to have the lovely smell of licorice without the black tongue, or the overload of calories from indulging in a feed of Allsorts or the thought that too much licorice will blow my blood pressure sky-high.

And, of course, that smell takes me back many years, to my introduction to licorice—and the time when I was literally picked up by the police.

Feasts from the Farm

Clams, Past and Present

My father, who was born a Newfoundlander but became an Islander after the Great War, enjoyed fish in any form, with shell or fin, and tried to pass on that love to his children. There was very little of the finny lot that I wouldn't try, although I did balk at cod cheeks and tongues, which Dad considered a real treat. Some days, when he was working extra-long hours and wouldn't arrive home until late at night, Mother would leave such a dish on the back of the stove to keep warm, to gladden his stomach and his spirits.

It was Dad who introduced us to a real honest-to-goodness clam bake. I have read of mixtures of potatoes and corn, and different kinds of fin fish as well as clams, all steamed together with seaweed, under the name of clam-bake. For us, it was clams and clams alone. They were cooked over a fire, on flat metal trays that I think Dad had scrounged from a friend who had a greenhouse. The clams were just baked in their own juice, which had a strong taste of iodine from the sea. Dad was a great believer in the benefits of iodine in that form (as well as in the virtues of cod liver oil!).

The clams we enjoyed as youngsters came from a shore that no longer exists; the shore was filled in for development and a tank farm was set up there. The clams had a number of common names—littleneck, mud clams, and the very inelegant, yet descriptive, piss clams. When they feel the vibrations of approaching feet, they can contract their neck muscle to squirt a water jet while retreating into the sand. The feet could be human or animal. Recently, while reading a description of early European settlement along the Atlantic coast of America, I saw an account of pigs being allowed on the shore to root out and eat clams. Pigs' noses are certainly powerful; their digestive systems must be, too, if they can handle shell in their diet.

Some mammals can handle much heavier shell. At one time there were walrus in Northumberland Strait, and they ate bar clams. At the mouth of the Tryon River there is a great area of sand bars known as the Tryon Shoal. A little farther along the Northumberland Strait there are lobster, herring, and scallop spawning grounds. At one time these parts of the Strait teemed with many forms of marine life, among them walrus (sea cows) in great numbers. They could dig out the bar clams with their long strong tusks, and crush the shells with their powerful molars, then haul themselves onto the sandy shore of Tryon Point to rest in the sun. That was five hundred years ago. The walrus are gone from the Strait, remembered only in place names such as Sea Cow Head and Sea Cow Pond. The shoal remains, but it is more often called the Tryon Clam Bars (no resemblance to Shellfish Bars in the big cities!).

A full-grown bar clam is a heavy beast, large enough to cover an adult-sized palm. We often thought it might be a good idea to shuck the clams as they were dug, and leave the shells on the sand, but it always seemed more important to get clams dug before the tide came in. I found it easiest to detect the clams just as the tide was turning. These clams have a relatively short, two-part siphon. One of the tubes takes in water with small particles of food, and the other carries out wastes. As the water returns, the ends of the siphon appear at the surface of the sand, looking like two little eyes. That's how I preferred to find them.

Those clam bars were a great place for me to think about days gone by. As I stood there I could see far up the river valley on one side of me and the mainland on the other. In my mind's eye I could see native peoples coming across the land bridge that connected the Maritime Provinces when the glaciers retreated. These people travelled up the valley for several miles before camping. Their presence has been authenticated by the finding of a chalcedony spear point in Tryon from 10,600 years ago, the same period of the Debert settlement in Nova Scotia. Their visits continued over a long span of time before they began living here year-round. Eventually the purpose of the summer visits was to stock up on food for the winter. Shellfish—bar clams, mud clams, quahogs, razor clams, mussels, maybe even oysters—were dried over fires and carried back to their winter quarters on the mainland. The dried product would, I think, be tough, but soaked and simmered a long time it would be edible and quite nutritious.

Bar clams have a large, triangular, very strong pseudopod (foot), which provides digging power by expanding and contracting. Its hinges are two white muscles, similar to those of scallops. There are some who eat only the muscles, but we use all but the stomach. Euell Gibbons, the American wild-food gatherer-writer, once wrote that "the muscular foot which is tough as a piece of harness leather is very poor fare." He quoted other writers as saying the clams were "good only for fish bait" and "unfit for human consumption." These writers were quite wrong. The foot is tough, but put through a food chopper, mixed with onion, salt and pepper, made into cakes, floured, and pan-fried, they are really good eating.

We don't can clams anymore. Instead I steam, clean, and pack them in their own juice, then freeze them. A few we will freeze from the raw state, to be fried for an extra-special treat in the winter.

Everett still goes to the shore for clams for us, but, since breaking an ankle a few years ago, I have been unable to join him, and I miss the experience. On a soft spring evening, with just a little breeze, the full-moon tide at its lowest, it was a joy to be there.

Foods for Winter

Preparing food that could be stored for winter use occupied a lot of time for the farm family, mostly the female part—until about the 1950s—when paved roads made it easier to get to the store and electricity fostered the use of home freezers. Everett's family, on both sides, were farmers in Tryon since the 1700s, and my maternal ancestors from their arrival in the 1800s. So the information I am passing on to you came from generations of people who depended on their home-prepared foods to keep them through the winter.

My Grandma MacBeth had a big barrel churn. She made a lot of butter, some of which was sold in one-pound blocks called "prints." But more of it was packed into five-gallon crocks and stored in the cellar, to be used in the winter when the cows went dry.

The same kinds of crocks stored eggs. In the fall, when newly threshed grain was available, eggs were layered among fresh oats. They would keep well-stored in a cool place. I can barely remember being allowed, as a small child, to reach down very carefully through the slithery oats to find the eggs nestled there.

Those five-gallon crocks had many uses. In the fall, when the pigs were slaughtered, some cuts were cured in brine, some might be "dry-cured," and some, particularly chops and small roasts, were baked in the oven and packed in a crock, with melted fat poured on top. The crock would then be covered, and down to the cellar the meat would go. Crock covers were prone to breaking, so if they were in short supply, well-greased heavy brown paper would be tied on.

Grandpa and Granny Howatt used the dry-cure method, which, as it went along, became fairly liquid. I know that from first-hand experience. Everett and I didn't raise any pigs, but one year we bought half a pig from a neighbour. One day, he brought the somewhat bloody carcass in and plunked it down on the kitchen table—a sight that turned our son off pork for several years. With Grandpa's help, we cut the side into recognizable portions and prepared the curing mixture, a combination of pickling salt, brown sugar, and saltpetre, which we rubbed on the meat for several days. Gradually a liquid formed, which was poured over the meat until it was considered cured. We then dried if off, wrapped it in cotton, and hung it in a cool place.

On most farms, after the best pieces were dealt with, the housewife boiled the pig's head, with or without the addition of beef parts, removed the meat, chopped it finely, added onions and spices, and then boiled the meat again with some of the liquid. We called the result "potted meat." In Europe it would be called "brawn" or even "souse meat," a name that came to the Appalachian region with early English settlers, and was still in use there in the 1970s.

On my uncle's farm, the potted meat was put in glass sealers and cooked in a big boiler. It then would keep indefinitely. Made into sandwiches with homemade bread and home-churned butter, potted meat would be a real treat for lunch for folks working at the hay away from the home farm. Even Everett and I made potted meat from our half-a-pig. It was good and we enjoyed it, but it was a lot of work. Nowadays we make do with an Island-made commercial product.

Potted meat wasn't the only labour-intensive winter preparation in days gone by, of course. Beef, chicken, peas, and beans were all cooked in glass jars. The meat required about three hours of boiling, the vegetables quite a bit less. I can remember helping my aunt pod several bushels of peas for processing.

Grandpa and Granny Howatt had a small orchard, as did most farmers of the day. Some of the autumn apples, though of good quality, would not keep well, so they would be prepared for drying. The apples were peeled, cut in a spiral, dipped in lightly salted water to reduce any discolouring caused by oxidation, and then threaded on a string and hung behind the stove to dry. On reaching a leathery stage, they would be put in a flour bag and stored in a relatively dry place. Everett remembers helping at that chore. We still have his grandmother's machine that cored, peeled, and sliced the apples, all in one operation.

When I prepare crushed strawberries for winter, I mash two quarts of berries with a potato masher, add a half-cup of sugar and store them in plastic containers in the freezer. No finesse to that. Everett's aunt, on the other hand, had a very particular way of preparing berries. She crushed one berry at a time on a china plate, using a silver fork. Nothing else would do. She mixed the raw fruit with twice the volume of sugar, poured the mixture into glass sealers, and set the crushed berries in a cool place. There was no processing involved; the heavy sugar content was supposed to prevent fermentation. The resulting product was considered a real gourmet treat, used on very special occasions.

My relatives had a method of preserving blueberries that I have not heard of elsewhere. Some summers, there were more blueberries available than could be eaten or made into jam. My family would pour the berries into quart sealers and cover them with freshly drawn cold water and a teaspoon of salt. Once again, no processing. The fruit would keep indefinitely and was quite acceptable in puddings and pies. When I came to live in Tryon, my new family was somewhat skeptical about such a product, but soon became believers. I used that method for years until we bought a freezer.

Sauerkraut wasn't part of the diet in my childhood home, but when I came to live in Tryon I soon learned how to make it, cook with it and like it. A few years ago, we bought ourselves a small oak barrel just for sauerkraut. Though some may add water, vinegar, wine, red peppers, and black pepper to the cabbage, we made ours the original way, just sliced cabbage and coarse salt, pounded into the barrel and kept at a fairly constant temperature to allow the stuff to "work." The pounding packs the cabbage and releases liquid, which dissolves the salt. The resulting brine should rise above the cabbage during fermentation. Once the fermenting is done and the liquid reabsorbed, we store the kraut in a cool place. In fact, it can even be frozen; my husband remembers enjoying it with ice crystals still in it. The last time we used our oak barrel, the brine did not rise. Our son had pounded the cabbage so vigorously, a stave had come loose at the bottom and the liquid had seeped out behind the stove. No sauerkraut that year. Since then, we've switched to a five-gallon plastic bucket.

The bucket may not be traditional, but the practice of making sauerkraut is a custom that goes back hundreds of years. Cabbage, from which sauerkraut is made, was native to the Mediterranean area but thrived in cooler countries farther north, where it became a staple food. How to store it over the winter was a problem. It could be stored, wrapper leaves and all, in outdoor pits, or it could be suspended from its own stem in a cellar. Or it could be made into pickled cabbage—sauerkraut in German.

In the early 1700s, mercenaries from the German state of Lunenburg, who served with British forces in the Maritimes, introduced sauerkraut-making to this part of Canada. When the Germans were disbanded, they settled on the South Shore of Nova Scotia, naming their community after their homeland, and that area became the hub of sauerkraut-making. In later years it was concentrated around Tancook Island, where people developed strains of cabbage better suited to their needs than some of the regular commercial varieties.

When Prince Edward Island storekeepers began selling sauerkraut in barrels, Islanders developed a taste for it and began making their own, even if they happened to have a Scots or Irish background. Sauerkraut produces lots of juice, which reminds me that the Pennsylvania Dutch supposedly valued the juice as a cure for a hangover. I prefer to think of sauerkraut as a delicious food, either on its own or as an ingredient that can be used in somewhat surprising ways.

Many people think of sauerkraut only in association with pork in various forms, so when I tell my cooking friends I use it to make a delicious moist chocolate cake, I get looks of great disbelief—until they try this recipe:

Sauerkraut Chocolate Cake

2-1/4 cups sifted all-purpose flour
1/2 cup unsweetened cocoa
1 tsp. baking powder
1 tsp. baking soda
1/4 tsp. salt
2/3 cup butter at room temperature
1-1/2 cups sugar
3 large eggs
1 tsp. vanilla
1 cup water or strong coffee
2/3 cup sauerkraut, rinsed, drained, coarsely chopped.

Combine first five ingredients. In another bowl cream the butter, gradually add sugar, and eggs one at a time. Add vanilla. Add liquid and dry ingredients alternately (beginning and ending with dry); stir in sauerkraut. Bake in two 8-inch pans, round or square, at 350 degrees F for 25 to 30 minutes. Fill and frost with mocha whipped cream or chocolate fudge frosting. I prefer to use raspberry jam between the layers and on top, then cover that with chocolate icing. Some good, winter or summer!

Associated with Ice

In the cellar of the house that Grandpa Howatt built, there is an oak ice-box, now unused. In our barn there is a large set of very heavy tongs, once used for handling blocks of ice. On a shelf in my living room, along with other dishes I treasure, there is a very special serving dish. At one time it had pride of place in Granny Howatt's china cupboard. These three things are related through their association with ice.

The ice-box was a nice-looking piece of equipment, made of varnished oak, with a zinc-lined compartment on top, from which air, cooled by a large piece of ice, would fall into the lower cupboard part. Shelves there held the milk, butter, eggs, and meat—foods that at one time would have been kept in a cold cellar, or even hung in a bucket in the well. That ice-box was a real convenience for the housewife.

Neighbours from the Point Road hauled their ice from a small pond about a mile away from our farm. A small dam kept out salt water from a tidal inlet, at the same time allowing fresh water from a small brook to build up enough depth to power a water wheel year-round, and supply ice in the winter.

The men in the family cut the ice by hand with a large saw in February or early March, when there was depth enough to make good-sized blocks. The men grasped the blocks of ice with those big tongs, and dragged them to a waiting sleigh. Then it was home to the ice-house, which was waiting with a thick layer of clean fresh sawdust, ready to cushion the ice. The blocks were packed in with sawdust around the walls and on top. Sometimes the building was double-walled, the space between the walls filled with seaweed or sawdust for extra insulation.

Everett knew the ice-cutting business at first hand—and foot and all the other parts. During my first year of teaching in a rural school, I boarded at the home of Everett's cousin and his wife. Everett's aunt and uncle had a house in the same yard. One weekend in October, Everett arrived for a visit with his relatives. That was our first meeting. After that, Everett began to visit his relatives more often. In February, he came for a couple of days to give his cousin a hand at cutting ice in a pond a short distance from the schoolhouse. The two men started sawing away, and Everett stepped on the cake he was working on. When the men cut the cake free, Everett and the block of ice disappeared into the icy water. Thankfully, the pond wasn't deep, and there was no current. Everett soon popped up like a cork. His cousin was so amused he could hardly stop laughing long enough to help Everett out. They quickly drove to the house, with Everett standing on the back of the tractor. His clothes froze stiff, but he suffered no ill effects, other than lots of teasing for having his mind on the schoolhouse instead of the ice pond. He lost his saw, though. As far as we know, it is still in the pond.

One lovely summer weekend before we were married, I was visiting at Everett's home. His brother, sister-in-law, and little nephew were there, too. Granny decided to make ice cream, which she always started by making a boiled custard. When the custard was cool, she added pure cream and poured the mixture into the metal cylinder of the freezer. She then inserted the dasher, adjusted the top with its cranking handle, and set the cylinder into the wooden freezer and packed it with ice and coarse salt. Then the handle of the freezer had to be turned.

One of my old cookbooks claims that "with ice-cream freezer, burlap bag, wooden mallet or axe, small saucepan, sufficient ice, and coarse rock salt, the process neither takes much time nor patience." That might have been correct for that writer, but sometimes unforeseen things happen.

On that particular day, we were outdoors preparing the ice when Granny asked me to bring the custard from the pantry. The cream was added and the cranking began. Everyone took a turn, but, for some strange reason, the ice cream wasn't freezing. The mixture remained quite liquid. Granny began to think. She had made boiled salad dressing as well as custard that day. I had obviously brought out the dressing instead of the custard. The result was that we had to empty the cylinder and begin again. That was a hard day on the cream supply.

The procedure at Granny's was that, once ice cream was properly made and "ripened," she brought out her lovely serving plate. She ran hot water over the cylinder, slid the ice cream onto the plate in one whole piece, and carried it proudly to the table. There she sliced it and served it with a choice of sauces. As if that wasn't enough, the ice cream was usually accompanied by two cakes: an angel-food cake made with the whites of twelve eggs, and a sunshine cake, which used ten of the egg yolks, plus two whole eggs. The two remaining yolks probably went into something like the salad dressing.

Last summer, Everett and I stopped at a local service station to get gas. Two out-of-province vehicles drove in, and the male drivers bought ice for their coolers. The ice, in plastic bags, was in blocks, and wouldn't fit on top of contents in the coolers. We watched as the men swung the bags overhead, then whacked them on the pavement until the ice was broken enough to spread easily. We were amazed that the plastic didn't break during such treatment, and recalled the days of using an axe to break up ice in a jute bag. Those were the days when nobody knew anything about cholesterol, and eating butterfat and lots of eggs wasn't considered a health hazard—and ice cream could be enjoyed without a guilty conscience.

Granny's Recipe for Ice Cream
2 cups scalded milk
1 egg
1 tablespoon flour
1/8 teaspoon salt
1 cup sugar
1 quart cream
2 tablespoons vanilla

Mix flour, sugar and salt, add egg, slightly beaten, and milk gradually. Cook over hot water for 10 minutes, stirring constantly at first; should custard have curdled appearance it will disappear in freezing. When cool, add cream and flavouring; strain and freeze.

Ground Ivy and Hops

One of my earliest memories is of the day I picked a bunch of ground ivy and buttercup blossoms for my mother. I was three years old at the time. Those blue-and-yellow flowers were growing on the bank of a small stream known as Spring Park Brook. Before it was paved over and disappeared from sight, that little brook wandered under and around the streets of Charlottetown.

It was on the side of that brook, near Spring Park Road, that I first saw ground ivy. I didn't see it again until I married and came to live in Tryon. At first, I didn't recognize it because it can look different in different locations. Its flower remains the same, as does the general leaf shape, but its growth habits change. In a sunny spot, it can be a squat little plant only a few inches high. But give it moisture and shade, and it can grow into a thick mat with shoots three feet long. Not only that, it roots readily at each leaf node as it spreads. No wonder it is used as a soil stabilizer in some parts of the country.

Ground ivy is not native here. Coming to us from Eurasia, it has naturalized itself from Newfoundland to Ontario, and south into the United States. It had so many uses in the Old Country that I imagine it was brought here intentionally, rather than as a stowaway. Some accounts from the first century AD say that the Greek physician Dioscorides used a leaf tea for sciatica. About the same time, Galen, another Greek physician, wrote that the plant "would not only soothe inflamed eyes, but cure failing eyesight in one almost blind."

The principal use of ground ivy, however, seems to have been in making ale, the drink of most people in an age when water, at least in towns and cities, was hardly fit to drink. That explains several of the common names for ground ivy in England—ale hoof or tun hoof. The word "hoof" came from an Old English name for the plant, "hofe." Tun was a cask that would hold 252 gallons (Imperial measure). The plants served to clarify the newly made ale.

William Harrison, Anglican Rector of Radwinter, describes in his Description of England (1577), how his wife brewed enough ale for their household once a month. (I wish he had told us how many there were.) She started by mixing malted grains with 86 gallons of boiling water, then added a second 86 gallons, and finally a third. "Thereof," the rector explained, "we make three hogsheads of good drink as is meet [fit] for poore men as I am withal, whose small maintenance of fortie pounds a year may endure no deeper cut." That seems like a heavy chore for the wife, even with a servant to fetch and carry wood and water for the process.

It was during the reign of Henry VIII that hops were introduced into England by the Dutch, who had been using the plants as a flavouring for beer for a century. A little piece of doggerel from the reign of Henry VIII says:

> *Turkies, heresies, hops and beer,*
> *All came to England in one year.*
> (*From* Lost Country Life, *by Dorothy Hartley*)

That little rhyme refers to three memorable events: Turkeys, native to the Americas, were taken to Europe by the Spaniards; Henry VIII broke with the Church of Rome and began the Church of England (the heresies); and Dutch beer made with hops started competing with good English ale.

Hops did not receive a warm welcome in England. The Royal Brewmaster was warned not to add hops or brimstone to the royal ale; Henry didn't need anything to make him more rambunctious. Indeed, so suspicious of hops were the people of London that they petitioned Parliament against this "nuisance, hops." Later, during the reign of Queen Elizabeth I, an edict was issued against the use of "that pernicious weed, the hop."

In this part of the world, hops at one time provided yeast for bread-making. Both Everett's grandparents and mine had hop vines growing on their farms. Hops have separate male and female plants; only the female produces the papery cone-like flowers that are covered with yellow glands, almost like sticky pollen. The fresh flowers were boiled down, perhaps with a piece of sourdough starter added, thickened with corn meal, spread to dry, cut into cakes, and stored for later use.

Many of the farms around here had hop vines at one time, but, by the time I came to Tryon to live, they were all gone. It was much easier to buy Royal yeast cakes. I remember they seemed to have a gritty, cornmeal feel to them. But I wanted to try making some yeast, so I bought a hop vine, which was guaranteed to be a female plant. In its second winter, I was checking it out in December when I noticed big fat shoots poking out of the ground. I pulled soil over them to protect them, and they survived and grew well. In fact, they needed a tall trellis to support them. But no blooms appeared. The next year, no plant.

I still think I would like to try hops again, perhaps in a different location. If the hop vine would only grow as strong as the ground ivy plants, I'd have shoots to eat and lots of flowers, too. As it is, I pull out ground ivy by the yard, by the bushel. While I'm doing that, I remind myself that those little blue flowers, which enticed me to Spring Park Brook when I was very young, provide lots of nectar for our bees in early spring. Thank Heaven for small mercies!

Gifts from the Sea

After a storm in the old days, Grandpa Howatt used to leave home before breakfast to haul cartloads of seaweed from the shore. There was much competition for seaweed in those days, so to lay claim to a good windrow, he'd try to arrive before first light. Sometimes local farmers would fork as much seaweed as they could onto the bank of the shore before anyone else arrived, and would then stand guard over their precious stash, pitchforks at the ready, until they could get it all hauled home. Sometimes the farmers even came to blows.

Those were the days before commercial fertilizers became available, and seaweed was vital to the health of crops on the Island. For many generations of farmers living near the seashores, seaweed was also an important source of bedding for animals and winter banking for houses. Used as bedding, the seaweed would be incorporated into the manure, and would break down relatively quickly when spread on the land. Besides seaweed, that shore supplied Grandpa with finely ground oyster and mussel shells, which he would shovel into bags for his hens. In the days before farmers could buy grit, the calcium from the seashells strengthened the eggs.

In this country, more and more people are turning, or returning, to natural, unmodified foods in the search for good health—perhaps following the advice of Hippocrates, the Father of Medicine, who said, "Leave your drugs in the chemist's pot if you cannot cure the patient with food." One of those natural foods is dulse, another gift from the sea. It can be enjoyed as a snack of dried fronds or flakes, or used finely ground as a seasoning.

Recently I came across one writer's opinion of fresh dulse: "... tough and elastic, like chewing on a salted rubber band." It brought to mind a picture of my mother at the shore, trying to persuade us children to eat some seaweed with her. The words, "Try it, it's good for you," didn't work very well. The explanation that the iodine in it would prevent goitre didn't carry much weight either. That was many years ago. Now my daughter and I truly enjoy dulse in the dried form that is readily available in supermarkets. When our New Brunswick relatives bring us a large bag from the City Market in Saint John, we really indulge.

Irish moss, or carragheen, is another red algae that grows well in the waters around Prince Edward Island. (Near Waterford, Ireland, the seaweed is plentiful at a place named Carragheen; the substance extracted from the moss is known as carageenan.) It grows on rocks on the Atlantic coasts of both Europe and North America, on the English Channel, and on the North Sea coasts of Europe and Britain. On our Atlantic coast, it grows from Labrador to New Jersey.

Here on the Island, Irish moss is harvested in a number of ways. It can be picked from pieces brought in by the tides, especially after a storm, and left on the shore. That picking may not be easy because of other seaweeds, sand, and shells mixed in. On the western end of the Island, harvesters close to the shore use large rakes pulled by horses; farther out, they use boat-hauling drags. In days gone by, picking, sorting, cleaning, and drying moss kept many people employed, though rarely well-paid, even when a factory for buying the product was set up. There are problems now because another marine plant is taking over the beds, and a cheaper product is being brought in from the Philippines.

People have used Irish moss in many ways for hundreds of years—fresh or dried for blanc-mange and jellies; as a thickening for many foods long before cornstarch or commercial jelling products became available; and as an ingredient in bath gels and face creams. At one time, the moss was used as a soothing medicine for coughs and peptic ulcers; now it's a base for medicated ointments, an emulsifying agent for cod liver oil, and an ingredient in cosmetics, ice cream, canned milk, and chocolate milk.

Shortly after Everett and I were married, Granny Howatt introduced me to "Sea Moss Pudding," made the way generations before her had done. We picked moss from a windrow on the shore, washed it, used some fresh, and dried the rest for later. It was quite a few years before I actually saw a bed of Irish moss. One Sunday afternoon, Everett and I walked to the Point to sit in peace and quiet for a while, and to check out the bird life. A short distance away, a headland shelved out to the water, which was at very low tide. Instead of the usual sandstone-shale colour, the water had a flush of pretty red all over it. Everett climbed down to investigate, and shouted to me that the red substance was Irish Moss. He picked some, and we carried it home in the only container we had, an old pith helmet I was wearing. It had been my Dad's, well-used for many things, so being a container for Irish moss was nothing unusual. The Irish moss bed was quite new, as we hadn't noticed it before, and the moss was much prettier than what we would find mixed up on the shore. When we arrived home, I washed it and dried it on a tray in the plant room, and later used it for puddings.

Sea Moss Pudding

1/2 cup Irish moss. Wash in tepid water, pick over and put in double boiler with one quart of milk. Boil until it thickens when dropped on a cold plate. Add salt and strain, not allowing any moss to pass. Add flavour and turn into a mould.

Blueberries

My maternal relatives, with whom I spent many summers, had a second farm a few miles away from the home place. Known simply as "the other place," it had a woodlot that had been cut down at one time, but was growing up again in poplars, birch, maples, a few spruce, bayberry, and sweet-scented ferns. It was a wonderfully fragrant place, and blueberries grew there abundantly.

The second growth was not very thick, because my uncle had pastured sheep in the woodlot and adjacent fields for many years. Thanks to the sheep, picking was relatively easy. Paths were everywhere, trodden down by the sheep, so walking around the hummocks wasn't a problem. In fact, sitting in a path, and picking the fruit from the mounds all around us, seemed much easier than picking on a flat area. It was so very pleasant on a sunny summer day to be able to work in such surroundings.

The blueberries we picked would keep well in a cool place, so we ate many of them raw. The women in the family also made pies, grunts, cobblers, and cake. My favourite was blueberry cake, hot from the oven and slathered with butter. What bliss! As jam, I found blueberries quite bland, although sometimes they would be perked up with the addition of apples or late rhubarb. Some were preserved in salt water, a method I speak of elsewhere.

When blueberries were especially plentiful, we picked them for sale. The store in the nearest village acted as agent for Canada Packers, which provided the "shooks"—small crates, made of thin wood veneer—for the berries. When assembled, the crates held twenty-eight to thirty pounds of berries. They would be shipped long distances by railway.

One year, we got 32 cents a pound for our berries—a real fortune. But "easy come, easy go": one payday I spent my money at the berry-buying store, most of it on cigars for Dad, and a blueberry-coloured satin cushion for Mother, but no doubt also on candy for my cousins and me. The cigars were soon gone, but the cushion lingered for a long time, getting uglier as the years went by. Mother hung onto it loyally; I think it finally left the living room when I left home to teach in the country.

One day, we youngsters rode to "the other place" on the truck-wagon with my uncle. He had a potato field there that needed spraying. The horse-drawn sprayer was a big wooden affair on two tall metal wheels; cogs and pulleys attached to the axle provided the pumping action that forced the spray mixture through nozzles on a boom across the back of the sprayer. Two horses provided the power. The same two horses pulled the truckwagon carrying us and two large puncheons full of water, probably about 120 gallons.

With no gasoline engines to pump water, my uncle had hauled water for the sprayer from a brook, carrying bucket after bucket until the puncheons were full. To keep the water from sloshing out as we drove over the clay roads, he had covered the puncheons with large pieces of canvas.

As my uncle went about his spraying, we children picked berries. Eventually, the sky became overcast, and by the time my uncle had emptied the puncheons, the rain had started, so we had to leave the blueberry patch. To keep us dry, or relatively so, my uncle lifted us into the empty puncheons and pulled the canvas on top, leaving us just enough space to peek out. That turned the outing into a real adventure.

On another day, a bright sunny one, we were returning home in the truckwagon with the empty puncheons. Along the way, we met a local man who "roamed the roads." He picked and sold berries of any kind, from wherever he could find them, and had become used to picking fruit at my uncle's place. He also became quite annoyed when we did, too. The man stood by the side of the road and shouted at us, "Hope you get your barrel full of berries!"—meaning the opposite, of course. He still retained some of the Scots accent of his ancestors so we heard the word "bay-reece." That sentence, with that pronunciation, became a catch phrase in our family, often used, but certainly not in that context.

Our native peoples no doubt enjoyed the berries fresh, and pounded great quantities with meat and fat into pemmican for winter food. The juice, boiled into a syrup, was a remedy for diarrhea, and tea from the leaves was thought to be a blood purifier and a treatment for inflammation of the kidneys. The natives also considered a bark extract effective against disease organisms. I find these uses quite interesting in light of the present-day research into the benefits of eating blueberries.

When I first came to live in Tryon, where blueberries had never really been plentiful, Granny had a few places where some could be found. But then potatoes became the king crop all around us, and there were no headlands or fence rows left where blueberries could find a home.

Everett and I decided we would plant some high-bush blueberries. To get a quantity at a price we could afford, we had to import them from New Jersey. That meant much paper work and frustration, but eventually we had some plants to set out.

The bushes have never attained the size of those grown in Nova Scotia. Still we persist. For years, a boat-builder friend of ours brought us the shavings and sawdust from his shop. We would carefully spread that material, plus what fell from Everett's wood-turning lathe, around those bushes to try to give them the humusy conditions they like.

Trouble is, Blue Jays, Robins, Song Sparrows, and Waxwings all enjoy blueberries as much as we do, and they don't mind getting up early in the morning to pick them. Forget nets; they just frustrate human pickers. Humming lines aren't much better. Aluminum plates hung on lines along the row, a plastic owl that needed to be moved every day—we've tried those, too. All this in an effort to acquire some sweet, beautiful blueberries to pick on a warm summer day, as I did when I was a child.

Edible Lilies

Before Everett and I were married, my mother gave me a useful piece of advice: "Never eat a raw onion sandwich before going to bed unless your husband likes onions, too." I think the advice came out of her own experience, as she didn't like raw onions at all and Dad did. I lived with my parents during my last year of teaching school in the City before my marriage, and Dad and I often enjoyed a raw onion sandwich as an evening snack. By the way, you need the bread and butter to tame those powerful onion juices. As Everett discovered one day, eating a whole raw onion on an empty stomach can set your insides on fire.

The onion is a biennial bulb, one of the large lily clan known as alliums, which is itself a family of more than three hundred members, both edible and ornamentals. Native to southwest Asia, cultivated worldwide, the onion has escaped to become naturalized in some areas. Onions have a very long, interesting history. The name comes from the Latin word *unio*, signifying unity, the eternal oneness. The bulb was deified in Egypt. Its concentric circles, with no beginning or ending, were a sign of that oneness. It didn't remain just an object of worship in the temples, but was an important item of food. In a writing from 1375 BC, we read about a workman's food: "After his long day's labour his wife would await him with a frugal supper of bread and beer, lentils and onions."

According to the Greek historian Herodotus, "there was spent in this root ninety ton of gold among the Workmen. So lushious and tempting the Israelites were ready to return to Slavery and Brick-

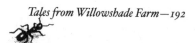

making for the love of them." His remarks are verified in the Book of Numbers in the Bible. The Children of Israel had been wandering in the desert for some years and were complaining bitterly: "We remember the fish we ate in Egypt for nothing, the cucumbers, the melons, the leeks, the onions and the garlic; but now our strength is dried up and there is nothing but this manna to look at."

Onions, or the lack of them, were actually the cause of what was probably the first recorded work strike in history. Ramose, Vizier (chief minister) to Pharaoh Amunhotep III, tried to pinch pennies on a pyramid-building job by cutting out the ration of onions, which formed a part of the workmen's wages. The workmen went on strike until the onion ration was returned. Some contend that garlic, not onions, was the cause of the uproar; probably it was some of both.

The onion's culinary cousin, garlic, wasn't a part of our growing-up diet. In fact, garlic was quite rare around here until after the Second World War: returning servicemen had been introduced to it and were more prepared to accept it. When the first European colonists came to North America, they found the native peoples using wild forms of garlic to treat afflictions ranging from snakebite to intestinal worms. Garlic wasn't new to those early settlers. Like the onion, garlic had been cultivated for thousands of years, widely used by Egyptians and Romans as both food and medicine. Either in raw form, or in a syrup made from boiling garlic cloves for half a day, garlic was taken to prevent infection and fight colds. When plagues ravaged Europe during the Middle Ages, people ate garlic daily as protection against catching the disease. In 1858, Dr. Louis Pasteur verified the antiseptic properties of garlic. According to *Magic and Medicine of Plants*, it is also a proven anti-spasmodic, and employed in the treatment of hypertension and arteriosclerosis.

In our house, we like both garlic and onions, raw, dried, boiled, baked, or fried—but not very often in a sandwich before going to bed.

Selected Bibliography

Angier, Bradford, *Field Guide to Medicinal Wild Plants*
(Harrisburg, PA: Stackpole Books, 1978).
Bishop, Carol, *The Book of Home Remedies and Herbal Cures*
(London: Octopus Books, Limited, 1979).
Bremness, Lesley, *The Complete Book of Herbs*
(Toronto: The Reader's Digest Association Canada, Ltd., 1989).
Brown, Demi, *Encyclopedia of Herbs and Their Uses*
(Montreal: R. D. Press, 1995).
Chidamian, Claude, *The Book of Cacti and other Succulents*
(New York: Doubleday and Company, Inc., 1958).
Culpeper, Nicholas, *Culpeper's Complete Herbal*
(London, W. Foulsham and Co. Ltd.).
Cumming, Roderick W., and Robert E. Lee, *Contemporary Perennials*
(New York: The Macmillan Company, 1960).
Edible Garden Weeds of Canada
(Ottawa: National Museums of Canada, 1980).
Fisher, Helen Field, and Gretchen Harshbarger,
The Flower Family Album
(Minneapolis, MN: University of Minnesota Press, 1941).
Free, John B., *Bees and Mankind*
(London: George Allen & Unwin Ltd., 1982).
Gibbons, Euell, *Stalking the Blue-Eyed Scallop*
(New York: David McKay Company, Inc., 1971).
Godfrey, W. Earl, *Birds of Canada, Revised Edition*
(Ottawa: National Museum of Natural Sciences, 1986).
Hartley, Dorothy, *Lost Country Life*
(New York: Pantheon Books, 1979).
Leighton, Ann, *Early American Gardens*
(Boston: Houghton Mifflin Company, 1970).
Magic and Medicine of Plants
(Pleasantville, NY: The Reader's Digest Association, Inc., 1986).
Michael, Pamela, *A Country Harvest*
(London: Peerage Books, 1986).
Nehrling, Arno, and Irene Nehrling, *Peonies Outdoors and In*
(New York: Hearthside Press, Inc., 1960).

Peterson, Roger Tory, *Field Guide to the Birds*
(Cambridge, MA: The Riverside Press, 1947).
Ramsay, Jane, *Plants for Beekeeping in Canada*
(London: International Bee Research Association, 1987).
Root, A. I., and E. R. Root, *ABC and XYZ of Bee Culture*
(Medina, Ohio: A. J. Root Company, 1910).
Shosteck, Robert, *Flowers and Plants, An International Lexicon*
(New York: Quadrangle/The New York Times Book Co., 1974).
Smith, A. W., *A Gardener's Book of Plant Names*
(New York: Harper and Row, 1963).
Song and Garden Birds of North America
(Washington, DC: National Geographic Society, 1964).
Stuart, Malcolm, Ed., *The Encyclopedia of Herbs and Herbalism*
(London: Arbis Publishing, 1981).
Tusser, Thomas, *Five Hundred Points of Good Husbandry*
(Oxford: Oxford University Press, 1984).
Water, Prey and Game Birds of North America
(Washington, DC: National Geographic Society, 1965).
Weiner, Michael A., *Earth Medicine—Earth Foods*
(London: Collier-Macmillan Limited, 1972).
Wild Animals of North America
(Washington, DC: National Geographic Society, 1971).

About the Author

A native Prince Edward Islander, Betty Howatt taught in rural and city schools before marrying and becoming a full-time farmer on land settled by her husband Everett's ancestors in 1783. Howatts' Fruit Farm—formerly called Willowshade Farm—on the Island's South Shore, is known across the Island for its quality fruit, vegetables, and honey. An outspoken activist on behalf of Island heritage, Betty was a long-time board member of the Prince Edward Island Museum and Heritage Foundation, and a staunch opponent of "The Fixed Link." A popular lecturer and guest speaker, she gives weekly lessons on Island plants and wildlife as part of her popular column on CBC Radio's afternoon program, "Mainstreet."